What Every Elementary Teacher Needs to Know About Reading Tests

(From Someone Who Has Written Them)

Charles Fuhrken

Stenhouse Publishers
Portland, Maine

Stenhouse Publishers
www.stenhouse.com

Credits

Pages 117–118: "The Question" from *Frindle* by Andrew Clements, reprinted with the permission of Simon & Schuster Books for Young Readers, an imprint of Simon & Schuster Children's Publishing Division. Text copyright © 1996 Andrew Clements.

Page 127: "The Rail-Splitter" from *A Three-Minute Speech: Lincoln's Remarks at Gettysburg* by Jennifer Armstrong, reprinted with the permission of Aladdin Paperbacks, an imprint of Simon & Schuster Children's Publishing Division. Text copyright © 2003 Jennifer Armstrong.

Page 137: "Squished Squirrel Poem" from *A Writing Kind of Day: Poems for Young Poets* by Ralph Fletcher (Wordsong, an imprint of Boyds Mills Press, 2005). Reprinted with the permission of Boyds Mills Press, Inc. Text copyright © 2005 by Ralph Fletcher.

Library of Congress Cataloging-in-Publication Data
Fuhrken, Charles.
    What every elementary teacher needs to know about reading tests (from someone who has written them) / Charles Fuhrken.
        p. cm.
    Includes bibliographical references and index.
    ISBN 978-1-57110-764-0 (alk. paper)
    1. Reading (Elementary)—Ability testing—United States—States.
2. Educational tests and measurements—United States—States. I. Title.
    LB1050.46.F84 2009
    372.48'2—dc22

                                                                    2008035258

Cover, interior design, and typesetting by Martha Drury
Manufactured in the United States of America on acid-free, recycled paper
15 14 13 12 11 10 09   9 8 7 6 5 4 3 2 1

To my earliest teachers—my parents, my sister, and my reading teachers at Orange Grove Elementary

Contents

Acknowledgments

This project has been a long time coming, and the vision for it has never been wholly my own. I have had the opportunity to sit and talk with new teachers whose questions about testing found their way to the pages—and in all hopes, those questions have been answered here. I have also had numerous conversations with veteran, exemplary reading teachers about testing, and their wisdom is most assuredly sprinkled throughout. Interviews with Peter Conforti, Nancy Gregory, Stephanie Heinchon, Elma Torres, Judy Wallis, and Karen Young, which informed another project, no doubt found their way into this book as well.

Nancy Roser deserves thanks because amid our marathon-long conversations in the fall of 2006, she wondered aloud if a future project for me might just be writing a book about testing. It was a moment that stayed with me as I wrote and rewrote since then.

I must thank two people who have been my teaching and writing models for years now—Sybil Lacey and Kemp Gregory. In addition, everything I know about assessment I learned from the best in the field, so I thank these numerous mentors, colleagues, and friends.

The teachers who allowed peeks into their classrooms—and whose students' remarkable work brings life to the activities in Section 4—were especially gracious. Thanks to you all: Peter Conforti, April Martin, April Mason, Christie Sumners, Kelly Taylor, Elma Torres, and Karen Young.

Thanks to Bill Varner, my editor, who got behind the project from the start, and to the editorial and production teams at Stenhouse, who responded to countless queries always with great cheer, especially Erin Trainer, Chris Downey, and Jay Kilburn.

Jeff Anderson provided frequent email encouragement. Carol Bedard and Chris Powell talked me to the finish line.

And importantly, thanks to John W. Jones, who, during my waves of worry, let me complain—but not too much.

Introduction

There is much that is mysterious about high-stakes testing. On a certain spring day, print-rich displays of student work and bulging bookshelves are covered up, rendering the classroom fairly sterile. "The test," which arrives in heavy cardboard boxes, is taken from one room to the next and placed in a teacher's closet that can be locked tightly and kept away from the human eye. When the testing period actually begins, the teacher becomes strange, reading directions in an official-sounding, test-proctor voice. Because it is test day, students, who are accustomed to collaborating with their peers and teacher, are now told that they must not look around, share their thinking, or ask questions. If they do ask questions, the teacher is required to greet their inquiries with the homogenized response, "Just do your best." Indeed, test taking is serious business, and it's no wonder that our youngest test takers are filled with anxiety about the peculiar work that has taken over the campus in the name of testing.

But the policies and procedures are not the only mysterious aspects of testing. The content of tests can be puzzling to students and teachers alike. While a state test purports to measure the curriculum, often the curriculum standards seem mysterious as well—written in code or so general in meaning that it seems impossible for teachers to know if their instruction will adequately prepare their students.

Furthermore, there seems to be a gulf between how reading skills and strategies are taught and understood in the classroom and how students are expected to apply those skills and strategies on a reading test. Test questions can be riddles for students, because the "test language" sounds very different from the ways in which students demonstrate their mastery of reading skills and strategies in the classroom. Students who cannot translate or access test language have a limited ability to demonstrate what they know (Kohn 2000; Valencia and Villarreal 2003).

Because testing has become pervasive as a result of the No Child Left Behind Act of 2002, a culture of panic is palpable in many, many school districts around the country. Test scores factor in to decisions about students' grade-level advancement and have become the basis for a district's accountability. Such pressure has led to a practice termed "teaching to the test," a departure from authentic reading instruction in favor of skill-based worksheets that are intended to help students creep toward a passing score (Firestone, Schorr, and Monfils 2004).

Yet reading teachers know that a steady regimen of test practice does not foster good reading habits and a lifelong love of reading in their students. Reading teachers know that school-mandated benchmarks and daily worksheet practice cause students to loathe reading and tests. And yet many of these teachers find themselves in a no-win situation: (1) they want their students to feel successful, but success is defined as a number on a score report; (2) they are not experts on testing, and they do not know where to turn for information about how reading standards are interpreted and assessed; and (3) they teach in a district whose philosophy is to "prepare" students with repeated practices with testing, which often reinforces students' lack of understanding of tests rather than increasing their understanding.

Purpose of the Book

The reality is that high-stakes tests are not likely to go away anytime soon. As a result, students need opportunities to learn about them. In recent years, teachers have approached tests as another genre to be read, explored, pondered, and questioned (Calkins, Montgomery, and Santman 1998). During the genre study of tests, students construct knowledge together about these unique sources of print. Teachers have rolled up their sleeves and wondered alongside their students about this thing called "the test"—without feeling that they had to give up their integrity in the process (Greene and Melton 2007; Conrad, Matthews, Zimmerman, and Allen 2008).

My belief is that teachers need better access to information about tests. Certainly the facets of test making are well documented (see, for instance, Downing and Haladyna's *Handbook of Test Development* [2006]), and state departments make their assessments as transparent as possible, which is why they release tests for teachers to study and use. But more often than not, the information about reading tests that is available to teachers is not packaged in a compact, ready-to-use, easy-to-understand form. If teachers knew more about how reading tests are made, how standards are interpreted, and how students can apply their knowledge of reading to the items that appear on reading tests, then teachers could spend much less time trying to figure out these tests and could feel less like servants to the dictates of their state assessment.

Making short work of informing teachers about what they need to know about state reading assessments to prepare their students means giving back to them their instructional time that is often wasted on test practice instead of valuable reading instruction. It's really this simple: The more teachers know about the content of reading tests and the strategies students can use to access test items, the quicker they can deliver that information to their students, not in the form of worksheets, but through focused test preparation that involves rich, lively, engaging reading and thoughtful, meaning-making experiences with their peers. How freeing.

About the Author

I have helped write reading tests—lots of them. This is rather ironic because I remember as a youngster reading dreadfully boring passages and wondering, with furrowed brow, "Who writes this stuff?" I had no idea that one day I would. I somewhat lucked into the profession, working as a freelance writer for a test publisher while teaching and attending graduate school. Now, over a decade later, I have served as a reading content specialist for several test publishers and have contributed to the development of many state assessments, including those of California, Georgia, Mississippi, Texas, and Virginia.

In the process, I worked with hundreds of teachers who were asked by their state departments to review the tests that I helped write. Those meetings were fascinating, because there was so much information-gathering and infor-mation-sharing happening at once. The reading specialists with the state departments and test publishers were interested in hearing the wisdom of the teachers who were teaching the very content that was being assessed on a state's test. The teachers took the opportunity to ask the burning questions they had about the assessment, and oftentimes, the information that was shared influ-enced their perspective and instructional practices. Countless times, I heard teachers say, "I wish I had known that." I came to realize that if teachers knew more about the construction and content of a reading test, they wouldn't be wasting their time or their students' time by having to take stabs at how to best prepare their students. Those conversations with teachers inspired this book.

Organization of the Book

The book is divided into four sections.

Section 1, "Building Understandings About Tests," is itself a test of sorts—it's only fitting to begin a book about testing with a test! In Chapter 1, commonly held beliefs about *test making* are presented, and in Chapter 2, commonly held beliefs about *test taking* are explored. Readers are asked to read statements about test making and test taking and decide if each is fact or fiction. The answers that follow the fact-or-fiction statements provide readers with a clear understanding of some of the realities and myths of testing.

Section 2, "Exploring Strategies for Reading Tests," takes a thorough look at the content of test items for the most commonly assessed reading standards on state assessments. This section is not designed around any particular state assessment. The truth is, reading is reading, no matter where students live! That is, although state tests might look different on the surface, the skills needed to master any state assessment are essentially the same. Section 2 divides those reading standards into strands and provides sample items and strategic approaches to answering those items. Before delving into this section, it is important to read the passage titled "Searching for an Idea" on pages 25–26. The discussions are based on items written for this passage.

Section 3, "Putting Strategies to Work," offers several passages and items that are similar to those featured on most state reading assessments for the elementary grades. Teacher guides are included so that teachers can use the materials to teach students those strategies explored in Section 2.

Section 4, "Demonstrating Understandings with Reading Activities," provides a multitude of resources—activities that relate to specific reading standards as well as helpful lists and books that can be incorporated easily into teachers' reading work with students.

Building Understandings About Tests

You can't believe everything you hear, and that goes for what people say about testing as well. There seem to be many truths and myths when it comes to testing, and these notions survive because they are passed from reading specialist to teacher, teacher to reading specialist, teacher to teacher, teacher to student, student to student, and so on. Truths can do little harm, but the myths that are perpetuated by well-meaning individuals often cause fellow educators to waste their instructional time with their students.

The purpose of the two chapters in this section is to build understandings about tests. Chapter 1 quizzes readers about some of the most common beliefs about *test making*—the ways in which tests are conceptualized and constructed by state departments of education and test publishers. Chapter 2 challenges readers to think about some of the most common beliefs about *test taking*—the strategies that students have come to think are the keys to unlocking multiple-choice test items.

Readers can consult the following list of terminology as needed while working through this section as well as the remainder of the book.

Terminology

Item: A test question with its answer choices. The terms *item* and *question* are interchangeable. The sample items presented throughout the book are multiple-choice items with four answer choices. Another common type is the constructed-response item (also called a short-response item, an open-ended item, or an essay question).

Stem: The beginning part of an item, which presents the task or problem. A *closed* stem ends with a question mark and is a complete thought. An *open* stem uses no punctuation at the end or uses a dash; the open stem and the correct answer together form a complete thought.

Options: The answer choices. The terms *options* and *answer choices* are interchangeable.

Correct answer: The one option that is clearly defensible as correct in a multiple-choice item.

Distractors: The three options that are incorrect in a multiple-choice item; also referred to as *wrong options*. (Sometimes spelled *distracters*.)

Passage: The text that test takers read prior to and while answering an item set. (There are many possible types/genres of texts.)

Standard: The core skill or criterion to which an item is written. Also called *objective, goal, expectation,* and *skill.*

Field test items: Items that collect data about students' performance but that do not count toward students' scores; they are often embedded in an operational form.

Operational form: The test form that purports to measure students' knowledge of curriculum standards and is the basis of students' scores. Also called a *live administration.*

Reporting category: A category within which standards are grouped for the purpose of reporting students' scores.

Examples

Standard: Analyze character traits.

In paragraph 1, how does the farmer feel?   ← *closed stem*
Options for closed-stem items usually begin with capital letters.

↓

distractors → A Puzzled
      → B Confident
      → C Eager
correct answer → D Angry

In paragraph 1, the farmer feels—   ← *open stem*
Options for open-stem items usually do not use capital letters.

↓

A puzzled
B confident
C eager
D angry ← *Options that are not complete sentences on their own may not have end punctuation; some assessments use end punctuation if the stem and the option together form a complete sentence.*

Chapter 1

Common Beliefs About Test Making: Fact or Fiction?

What's a book about testing without a test? So let's get to it—but you don't need pencils or a high level of test anxiety for this one! Below are five statements about the *test-making* process, which might or might not be true. Read each one, consider the contexts in which you may have heard each statement, and decide if you think it is fact or fiction.

1. "It's anyone's guess what students are expected to master for a state test."
2. "A state test is the responsibility of the state department of education, so teachers are essentially left out of the process."
3. "The test was harder this year than last year."
4. "All standards are assessed equally."
5. "Most multiple-choice items 'look' and 'sound' a certain way."

Now for the answers:

1. Fact or Fiction: "It's anyone's guess what students are expected to master for a state test."

Answer:

On any state's reading test, students are expected to demonstrate their mastery of the standards that compose the curriculum for a particular grade level. There can be no testing program without a curriculum. The curriculum is essentially the foundation upon which an assessment program can be built.

Therefore, the curriculum is the teacher's guide, the road map, for his or her instructional planning. In theory, then, students are expected to master the curriculum standards, so it's not "anyone's guess" and there shouldn't be any guesswork on the part of teachers. The often-heard complaint among educators, though, is that the standards themselves might indicate what students are expected to know, but they typically provide little information about how students are expected to demonstrate that knowledge. Teachers are often the ones left guessing about the kinds of items that students will encounter for a particular reading standard.

Section 2 is intended to bridge that gulf—the murky waters that lie between what students are taught about the reading standards and what students need to bring to the table in terms of reading skills and strategies in order to answer items correctly.

"It's anyone's guess what students are expected to master for a state test" is, in theory, fiction, but teachers might beg to differ. Therefore, the information in the following chapters is intended to take any guesswork out of preparing students for state reading tests.

2. Fact or Fiction: "A state test is the responsibility of the state department of education, so teachers are essentially left out of the process."

Answer:

While a state department of education is the administrator of an assessment program, teachers are a key part of the process from the beginning. One of the first steps of any new testing program is convening committees of educators to decide which aspects of the curriculum should be eligible for statewide assessment. Over the course of multiple days in these work sessions, educators examine and cull the curriculum to draft and organize test objectives. Educators are also asked to establish preliminary test blueprints, which specify test format and test length. (You can likely access your state's specific test-building process by consulting the education department's website.)

Once the state department puts the assessment framework in place, item development begins. During this stage, teachers might be involved as well. Because the content specialists employed by test publishers cannot possibly meet the passage and item needs of the state test by writing the content themselves, they obtain help—lots of it—by contracting with freelance passage locators (people who find published texts that can serve as appropriate test passages), passage writers, and item writers. Many of these freelancers are former or current classroom teachers.

In recent years, another approach for fulfilling item development needs has emerged. Some state departments want to actively involve their classroom teachers in the test development process rather than leave it largely up to test publishers. In work sessions, teachers who are currently teaching a particular subject and grade level are trained about constructing test items and then are responsible for writing the items for field testing. The result is said to be a test that more closely mirrors classroom instruction, because the item writers are the very people who are teaching the state's students.

Beyond contributing to the test development process as architects and authors, teachers have a fairly substantive voice in deciding the actual content of an operational test form. After items are field-tested, teachers meet in work sessions to evaluate the data sets for those field-tested items. Teachers are instructed on how to interpret the data in terms of content, fairness, bias and sensitivity, and so forth. After group discussions, teachers decide if items are eligible or ineligible for use in a live administration.

"A state test is the responsibility of the state department of education, so teachers are essentially left out of the process" is fiction, and educators can contact their state department about opportunities to participate in the test development process.

3.   Fact or Fiction: "The test was harder this year than last year."
Answer:

Thanks to psychometrics—a field of study concerned with educational and psychological measurement—all test forms for a particular subject area at a particular grade level and for a particular testing program maintain about the same level of difficulty in each administration.

The process of building a test is complex, but here's the short story: A test builder has a bank of items that has been field-tested. The items are assigned difficulty levels based on a number of factors, including the percentage of students who answered them correctly. When a test builder constructs a test form, the items selected must combine to reach a target difficulty level that remains constant from one test form to another. Now, here's where the plot thickens: The *difficulty level* must remain the same, but the *content* does not. While the items must come from the same reporting categories, such as "literal understandings" or "inferential thinking," the types of items selected may be different within a category. For example, one test form may contain more items related to drawing conclusions from the inferential thinking category, while another may contain more items related to predicting outcomes from this same category. If students find drawing conclusions to be more difficult than predicting outcomes, it may give the impression that that particular test form is more difficult.

In a perfect world, the test builder would always be able to hit the target from one form to the next. It's a lot like putting a puzzle together—a test builder might have to try many combinations of item content and item statistics before the test form matches the test blueprint and difficulty. Even so, there are instances in which the cut score (the minimum score to pass or reach a particular achievement level) must be adjusted in order to ensure that one form is the same difficulty as another. However, when a cut score has been raised or lowered slightly, the impression is that the test has been made harder or easier. It's actually quite the opposite! Adjusting the score slightly is often what makes one test form the same difficulty as another—which actually makes the test fairer to all students who take a test at a particular grade level in a particular content area, regardless of when they take it. (Admittedly, my explanation here drastically simplifies a complex process. Consult with your state department of education for more specific information about test equating and standard setting.)

"The test was harder this year than last year" is fiction. A testing program maintains the same level of difficulty across all administrations of the test, ensuring that all students must clear the same hurdle, regardless of which test form they take.

4.   Fact or Fiction: "All standards are assessed equally."
Answer:

All standards are not created equal—at least when it comes to assessing them.

State assessments do emphasize some standards more than others, as implied in the answer to the previous fact-or-fiction statement. Here's a recap: For the purposes of reporting students' scores, standards are placed in categories such as "literal understandings" or "inferential thinking." The number of items tested in each category is usually different. For instance, on a test with forty live items, ten might constitute "literal understandings" while thirty might constitute "inferential thinking." As a result, some standards are assessed more frequently than others.

Teachers are often surprised to learn that not all reading standards are "valued" in the same way. How state departments assign emphasis to the standards is usually not a secret, though. You can find information on what standards/skills are given more attention at a particular grade level by looking at a test blueprint, which may appear in information booklets released by the state; the front matter of released tests (possibly); and other information about test objectives found on most states' websites.

That said, perpetuating the myth that all standards are equal might not be a bad thing. If teachers take a well-balanced approach to teaching *all* standards of the curriculum, then students will be prepared for whatever items they encounter on the assessment. The opposite approach is not so appealing: that teachers emphasize or deemphasize certain reading standards based on how frequently they are measured on the state assessment. (Worse still is that those standards that are never assessed might go untaught altogether.) Such an approach is referred to as "teaching to the test"; it considerably narrows reading instruction and often leads to drill-to-skill (or "drill-and-kill") methods that involve worksheets and move students further away from the important work of engaging with texts.

"All standards are assessed equally" is fiction, but should not be a concern of teachers who wisely take a well-balanced approach to teaching all reading curriculum standards.

5.   Fact or Fiction: "Most multiple-choice items 'look' and 'sound' a certain way."

Answer:

Multiple-choice items are hard to mistake. Even young students learn quickly that multiple-choice items have a few features that remain consistent from one to another: a concisely worded stem along with several possible answers, all of which are concisely worded as well. Because test takers can expect items to look this way, they do not have to waste a lot of brainpower figuring out an item's basic structure.

Multiple-choice items tend to "sound" a certain way as well. When items are constructed, the writers do not simply write anything they want, any way they want. They follow guidelines that are provided by the test publisher, and these guidelines are quite similar regardless of the type or purpose of a test. Just search the Internet for "item writing guidelines" or grab any book about the test development process and you'll find that whether it's a state reading test, a nursing certification test, or a college entrance exam, there are agreed-upon ways to construct multiple-choice items.

Figure 1.1 shows some of the most common guidelines for constructing multiple-choice items. The guidelines and examples illustrate that item construction is fairly standardized, and test publishers and state departments scrutinize them to reflect specific qualities before they appear on a test form. Teachers might find it helpful to keep the guidelines and examples in Figure 1.1 in mind during their discussions with students about tests, mostly because students tend to develop their own ideas and theories about test items that might not be true. For instance, students might need to be taught explicitly that any noticeable differences in the options (such as in specificity or emphasis) are not intended as clues to the correctness or incorrectness of those options.

In essence, items have only one job to do—to allow students to demonstrate what they know. The standardization of item formatting and presentation helps ensure that students can focus their attention on *what* the item asks (the reading content) rather than *how* the item asks it (the construction).

"Most multiple-choice items 'look' and 'sound' a certain way" is fact, and constructing items to have a similar look and sound is entirely purposeful.

Options should not be visually appealing or distracting because of length or specificity.

Original	Revised
In paragraph 1, how does the farmer feel?	In paragraph 1, how does the farmer feel?
A Puzzled	A Puzzled by the animals' behavior
B Angry about the condition of the land	B Angry about the condition of the land

Options should not be visually appealing or distracting because of emphasis.

Original	Revised
In paragraph 1, how does the farmer feel?	In paragraph 1, how does the farmer feel?
A Puzzled	A Puzzled
B Angry and hopeless	B Angry

Options should not be imbalanced in terms of positives and negatives.

Original		Revised	
In paragraph 1, how does the farmer feel?		In paragraph 1, how does the farmer feel?	
A Satisfied	(+)	A Angry	(-)
B Confident	(+)	B Confident	(+)
C Eager	(+)	C Eager	(+)
D Cowardly	(-)	D Cowardly	(-)

Options should not use vocabulary that is above grade level.

Original	Revised
In paragraph 1, how does the farmer feel?	In paragraph 1, how does the farmer feel?
A Puzzled	A Puzzled
B Vexed	B Angry

Options should not be figurative or idiomatic in meaning.

Original	Revised
In paragraph 1, how does the farmer feel?	In paragraph 1, how does the farmer feel?
A Puzzled	A Puzzled
B Madder than a hornet	B Angry

FIGURE 1.1
Sample Test Item Guidelines

Options should not have multiple interpretations.

Original
In paragraph 1, how does the farmer feel?

A Proud (pleased or conceited?)

B Surprised (amazed or shocked?)

C Anxious (eager or nervous?)

D Thoughtful (caring or mindful?)

Revised
In paragraph 1, how does the farmer feel?

A Pleased

B Amazed

C Eager

D Caring

Options should not express the same idea with different words.

Original
Why does the farmer stare at the sky for two days?

A He hopes the skies will change soon. (correct answer)

B He is looking for a sign of rain. (correct answer)

Revised
Why does the farmer stare at the sky for two days?

A He has nothing else to do. (now incorrect)

B He is looking for a sign of rain. (now the only correct answer)

Item stems should not contain a clue about the correct answer.

Original
Which detail shows that the farmer is hopeful?

A He hopes it will rain.

Revised
Which detail shows that the farmer is hopeful?

A He expects rain to fall eventually.

Items should not provide clues to other items or assess the same idea.

This Item Clues This One →
Why does the hopeful farmer "stare at the sky for two days"?

A He is looking for a sign of rain.

← This Item Clues This One
Which idea shows that the farmer is hopeful?

A He stares at the sky for two days.

FIGURE 1.1
Sample Test Item Guidelines *(continued)*

Chapter 2

Common Beliefs About Test Taking: Fact or Fiction?

Yes, another test—same format, different content. This time, there are nine statements about *test taking*, which might or might not be true. Read each one, consider the contexts in which you may have heard each statement, and decide if you think it is fact or fiction.

1. "In a test item, there are two options that are correct, and students have to choose the best one."
2. "Process of elimination is a good test-taking strategy that all students can understand and use."
3. "Some items provide clues about the answers to other items."
4. "Many times, the longest option is the correct answer."
5. "When running out of time, choose C."
6. "When in doubt about the answer, choose C."
7. "Do not choose an option that contains the words *all*, *always*, or *never*, because that option will never be the correct answer."
8. "Your first instinct is the right answer."
9. "Even people who don't consider themselves to be good test takers can get better at taking tests."

Now for the answers:

1. Fact or Fiction: "In a test item, there are two options that are correct, and students have to choose the best one."

Answer:

Standard multiple-choice items contain four options—one correct answer and three incorrect choices. Items are not constructed so that there is one correct answer, one option that is really close to being correct but isn't, and two choices that are clearly incorrect.

Perhaps this myth has been perpetuated because test-item data do sometimes show that one incorrect answer choice draws more students than the other two. Consider this: Most students have gotten a test back from their teacher and kicked themselves because they had a question narrowed down to two options and then picked the wrong one. Test data show that students are typically pretty good at eliminating at least one answer choice as being "unattractive"—or really, really wrong! With a little thought, students often can eliminate yet another option of the three remaining. That leaves two answer choices. Is it by design that the one remaining incorrect choice is more compelling than the other two incorrect choices? Absolutely not. But when writing any item, it is often difficult to find three incorrect ideas to present, so some seem more sensible than others.

For every item, then, there is one correct answer choice and three incorrect. The correct answer must be clearly defensible, and the incorrect choices must not be arguably correct in any way. Test items are scrutinized by the test publishers that produce them, the state departments that review them, the committees of teachers that determine if the items are acceptable for testing, the students who answer them, and the public who view them in various documents released by the state departments. While there are occasions in which errors do occur, under no circumstances do test makers believe that fair items can have two correct responses, one of which is subjectively deemed better than the other.

"In a test item, there are two options that are correct and students have to choose the best one" is fiction.

2.   Fact or Fiction: "Process of elimination is a good test-taking strategy that all students can understand and use."

Answer:

Process of elimination—the strategy of eliminating one option at a time until only one remains—often gets a bad rap. The bad rap likely developed as a result of students' justifying their choice for an answer simply by saying they ruled out the other options. Teachers don't want to hear that. Teachers want to hear that students reread a section of a passage and located the information. Or that they used what the author said and what they could infer about that information to select the answer. Or that they used a combination of other strategies that have been taught to them.

But the truth is that all test takers use process of elimination, either intentionally or unconsciously, to settle on one answer for a multiple-choice item. It's inevitable in a multiple-choice item that offers four possibilities to narrow those four to three, those three to two, and those two to one. The hitch is whether students eliminate those options because they "don't sound right," or whether the students can find good reasons—text-based reasons—to eliminate them.

For young, nervous, or otherwise reluctant test takers, process of elimination as a strategy can actually be a good confidence booster. Because having to read and distinguish four options can be overwhelming, being able to eliminate one or more of the options can help students feel that they are well on their way to arriving at the correct answer.

"Process of elimination is a good test-taking strategy that all students can understand and use" is fact, but the effort that students put into thinking through all options of a test item certainly affects how useful the strategy is.

3.   Fact or Fiction: "Some items provide clues about the answers to other items."

Answer:

It is rare that items are clearly "clued" in such a way that one item contains information that blatantly gives away the answer to another. But because many items must be written for each standard to maintain a testing program, items sometimes repeat content in various ways. For example, a character-motivation item might ask students to recognize that a character is excited about an event, while the wording of a conclusion item might hint that the character is excited. Thus, the conclusion item provides a hint about the character item—but only for students who pick up on it!

The bottom line is that item clueing is usually eliminated at some point during the review process by the test publisher, state department, and educator committees. So, the odds of finding the answer to an item within another item are not in the students' favor. Students would waste their time by purposefully searching for instances of item clueing. And those students who are savvy enough to find item clueing most likely don't need the extra help!

"Some items provide clues about the answers to other items," might be fact, but clueing happens much too infrequently—and usually too subtly—to matter.

4.   Fact or Fiction: "Many times, the longest option is the correct answer."

Answer:

Reading items involve language, naturally—and the number of words that it takes to express an idea varies considerably. As a result, sometimes the longest option is the correct answer. And sometimes the shortest option is the correct answer. And sometimes neither the longest nor the shortest option is the correct answer.

To avoid drawing students' attention to the length of options, some state assessments order the options in ascending fashion such that the shortest option is always A and the longest option is always D. There's some wisdom to the method—students are less tempted to select an answer based on visual differences.

Furthermore, during the review process, the test publisher, state department, and educator committees consider the length of an item's options and rewrite options as needed so that no option is substantially different in length. So, the reason a longer option appears in an item is because more words are needed to express that idea sufficiently—regardless of whether that idea is right or wrong. Students should know that the length of an option has nothing to do with whether it is correct or incorrect.

But you don't have to take my word for it. Just take a form of any state's released test, choose the longest option for every item, and then grade it using the key. The result will most assuredly not be a passing score.

"Many times, the longest option is the correct answer" is fiction.

5.   Fact or Fiction: "When running out of time, choose C."
Answer:

Consider this scenario: A student has one minute left before time is up but still has four items to answer. If this student chooses C for all four items, he or she might get at least one item correct.

Now consider a different approach: For the last four items, the student bubbles in A, then B, then C, and then D. If the correct answers are B, then D, then A, then A, this student gets all four items wrong. By choosing C for all four items, the student increases the odds of getting at least one item correct.

For state assessments that are timed, students do need a good strategy when there is so little time left that they must select answers without even having the opportunity to read the items.

But there's nothing magical about option C! Test forms usually have a fairly even distribution of As, Bs, Cs, and Ds. So, technically, the advice should be, "When running out of time, choose A, B, C, or D and stick with it" rather than, "Choose C and stick with it."

"When running out of time, choose C," is neither fact nor fiction, but it is good advice for timed assessments.

6.   Fact or Fiction: "When in doubt about the answer, choose C."
Answer:

As mentioned above, a certain mystique about option C has arisen in recent years. Option C has become "the chosen one," but without good reason, because test forms usually have a fairly even distribution of the answer options.

The real trouble with this statement is that students have come to believe that at the first sign of uncertainty, they should select option C and move on. Clearly, this means that these students abandon the approach of using their reading strategies to consider each answer choice, narrow the choices, and then choose the best option based on the evidence they can mount for it. Furthermore, if students do make the effort and can narrow the options down to two, the advice "When in doubt about the answer, choose C" gives students the impression that C is probably the answer. Either way, option C is given much more consideration and power than it deserves!

"When in doubt, choose answer choice C" is fiction, plain and simple.

7. Fact or Fiction: "Do not choose an option that contains the words *all, always,* or *never,* because that option will never be the correct answer."

Answer:

Never say never!

It is difficult to pinpoint the origin of this advice. Teachers have explained to me that it came from the frustration of trying to help young children distinguish fact from opinion. Teachers instruct students that descriptive adjectives (for example, *prettier, friendliest*) and absolutes (for example, *always, never, all*) are "opinion or judgment words." So, the advice pertains to opinion items and, on the surface, makes some sense. Consider these statements, which are clearly opinions: "A rainy day is *always* more depressing than a sunny day" and "*Never* let them see you sweat."

Unfortunately, the advice doesn't hold up well. Think about this: There is scientific evidence to prove the statements "A bolt of lightning *always* precedes a clap of thunder" and "*All* gorillas are born with hair." There are also facts that don't require scientific evidence: "December is *always* the last month of our calendar year."

This advice, then, is specific to fact-opinion items, and yet there are many exceptions. A serious problem results for students who tend to overgeneralize and come to believe that whenever they encounter the words *all, always,* or *never* in an option in *any* item, that option is automatically wrong. What's frightening about the advice is that those supposed opinion words are used frequently in our language. Consider these sentences: "Kristopher has *always* enjoyed raising animals" and "Kristopher was *never* late for football practice this season." If these sentences are the details in the passage that support the correct answers to items about character motivation, students who think they should dismiss options that contain these words will get those items wrong.

"Do not choose an option that contains the word *all, always,* or *never,* because that option will never be the correct answer" is fiction.

8. Fact or Fiction: "Your first instinct is the right answer."

Answer:

Intuition is a powerful thing in life—and probably in testing as well.

The answer choice that "hits home" or is your "gut reaction" has often been said to be the correct answer. Many of us have learned that lesson the hard way: We have all wanted to kick ourselves when we received a test back from the teacher and realized that at one point, we had written the correct answer, erased it, written something different, and gotten it wrong as a result. But the reality is that we don't often pay attention to the times when we had written an *incorrect answer*, erased it, written something different, and gotten it *correct* as a result. Usually, those occasions are less noticeable because when we receive a test back from the teacher, we don't take notice of those questions we answered correctly—we're too busy kicking ourselves for the ones we answered incorrectly!

Nonetheless, the advice seems pretty harmless, if used as *one* gauge rather than the *only* gauge for determining the correct answer. Teachers have long grumbled about how young test takers do not read and consider all four answer choices. Students can find it hard to resist the temptation to mark the first answer choice that makes some sense. Sometimes that means students read option A, mark it, and move on without even considering the other options. These students misinterpret the advice "Your first instinct is the right answer" as "Mark the first thing that makes sense." Perhaps the advice needs to be reworded a bit: "After reading and considering the four choices, your first instinct might be the right answer" or "Read all answer choices because one might stand out to you more than the others."

That said, perhaps the real reason that your first instinct is often the right answer is because you are not conscious of the logic and reasoning skills you are using to read, understand, and consider the choices. It's not your gut that is telling your brain that a particular choice is correct. It's your brain that is telling your gut that the choice is correct!

"Your first instinct is the right answer" is fiction, but it is probably harmless advice when not misused.

9.   Fact or Fiction: "Even people who don't consider themselves to be good test takers can get better at taking tests."
Answer:

The age-old advice that practice makes perfect might need a little rethinking. Perhaps it is truer that bad practice makes for reinforcement of the wrong kinds of thinking and action. Good practice makes for better results and clearer kinds of thinking and action.

Bad practice—in terms of preparation for tests—is usually obvious. When a teacher's once balanced and comprehensive instruction narrows to include only those objectives that will appear on an assessment, that's bad practice. When once lively and engaging reading activities are replaced with drills and worksheets—that's bad practice.

But good practice is not necessarily devoid of discussions about assessment. Teachers shouldn't be so fearful of "teaching to the test" criticisms that they try to swing their instructional practices so far to the other side of the continuum that students are totally off-put when assessment week arrives in the spring. After all, students who have little experience with tests can feel displaced come test day. Students can become confounded because they have been in a classroom for a year in which the teacher invites and accepts a variety of responses from students' discussions of literature, but then on test day, that same teacher tells students that they must pick only one answer—the "correct" one.

When students read, strategize, and discuss test items, they become better prepared to demonstrate what they know about reading. When teachers help students think about and think through test items (especially particular types of test items), teachers are strengthening students' skill at negotiating the many ideas that confront them in a given reading passage and item set.

This type of focused test preparation is not at all like "teaching to the test." It looks different, sounds different, and feels different. It is not at all about barraging students with photocopied passage and item worksheets in which students work silently, have their work graded, and continue the routine until a certain score is achieved; the result of such a daily grind is that students spurn reading of any kind.

Instead, the kind of preparation that I am suggesting has teachers and students thinking and talking together about the reading standards. Teachers can gain access to students' understandings and misunderstandings so that lively and engaging activities can be used to redirect misunderstandings, strengthen existing ideas, and foster new ones. (See Section 4 for activities that are intended to invite students to think and talk about the reading standards that appear on most state tests.)

"Even people who don't consider themselves to be good test takers can get better at taking tests" is likely fact—when they have good opportunities to prepare. When teachers become more knowledgeable about test making, test taking, and test content, their students are the wiser for it.

Exploring Strategies for Reading Tests

This section is designed with two questions in mind:

1.   What is tested on most states' elementary reading assessments?
2.   What strategies can students use to answer those reading items?

The truth is that reading tests are mostly the same. No matter how a particular state's curriculum standards and test objectives are worded, students essentially encounter the same types of reading items for the same types of reading standards.

To make exploring the test content and reading strategies manageable, more than thirty of the most commonly assessed reading standards have been grouped into six strands. Each chapter in this section is devoted to one of these strands: Chapter 3, "Vocabulary Development," Chapter 4, "Important Ideas," Chapter 5, "Literary Elements," Chapter 6, "Literary Techniques," Chapter 7, "Interpretations," and Chapter 8, "Text Matters." Sample items and strategic approaches for answering those items are presented. These strategies are designed to be used individually or in combination. Oftentimes, more strategies are offered than students need, but the intent is to be as comprehensive as possible when presenting strategies that work. After all, students are empowered when they have many strategies and tools available to them and have learned when and how to apply them. Furthermore, although all the sample items are written in a multiple-choice format, students can use the strategies offered for other formats as well, such as with open-ended items. And for ease of reading, all the options in the sample items appear as ABCD, even though many states' actual test items follow an alternating pattern of ABCD and FGHJ.

The passage that follows, "Searching for an Idea," represents a typical elementary-grade test passage and is the basis of the sample items and discussions about the strategies, so read this passage first and consult it as needed while working through the chapters in this section.

Sample Passage

Searching for an Idea

1   Monica had been sitting at the kitchen table for more than an hour. She thought if she <u>concentrated</u>, she would come up with an idea. She had been thinking hard, and still she had not thought of anything. She sighed heavily when she looked down at the blank page in her notebook.

2   "I'm going to <u>fail</u> the fourth grade," she told her dad. Monica felt a knot twist tightly in her stomach. She was almost in tears now.

3   "What do you mean?" her dad asked.

4   Monica told her dad about her big assignment. Her class had been reading all kinds of poems. Now each student had to write a poem. It was due tomorrow.

5   "I can't write a poem. It's too hard," Monica said.

6   Usually Monica's dad was her homework helper. But this time, he seemed busy with other things. "You are good with words," her dad said. He smiled and walked away.

7   Monica couldn't believe what she heard. She often liked to have her dad's <u>guidance</u>. She thought he would want to write the poem with her.

8   Seconds later, Monica <u>burst</u> into her older brother's room. "I have to write a poem for school," Monica said. Then she had an idea. "If you write it with me, I'll do your kitchen chores tonight," she added. Monica knew her brother Ben hated to wash dishes.

9   Ben snatched Monica's notebook from her. He made a few scratches and then pitched the notebook back. He had written:

Roses are red.
Violets are blue.
Get out of my room!
I'm DONE WITH YOU!

10   Shooing her away, Ben put his headphones back in his ears. Monica should have known not to <u>bother</u> him while he was listening to his music.

11   Then she had another thought. She called her friend Sara and asked her what she was writing about.

12   "I'm writing about my aunt. She is so funny," Sara said. That didn't help Monica. Monica couldn't think of any humorous people she wanted to write about. Sara tried to help with other <u>suggestions</u>. "What about a place you've been or something you've read about?" Sara asked. Monica thanked Sara and hung up the phone. Still, nothing interested Monica.

13   A little while later, Monica's dad entered the kitchen again. "Is that poem written yet?" he asked.

14   Monica sat <u>speechless</u>. She simply held up her sheet of paper. There was still nothing on it.

15   "Why don't you come with me then," her dad said. "We'll try to find an idea on the way to the grocery store."

16   On the ride there, Monica stared out the window. She saw people talking on street corners. There were houses and tall buildings.

17   Monica could hear her teacher's words in her head: "You can write about anything." But Monica had nothing to say about the things around her.

18   Then Monica's dad drove the car up to an empty field.

19   "Why don't you write about this," Monica's dad said.

20   "About what?" Monica replied.

21   "Write about what you see," he said.

22   Monica sat still and stared ahead, pondering why her dad wanted her to look at the empty field. Monica then looked at him strangely.

23   "There's nothing happening here, Dad," she said. "There are no children playing. There are no flowers growing."

24   "Maybe that's what you should write!" he answered.

25   Monica looked out across the field again. Soon, thoughts danced in her head, and she struggled to get them all on paper quickly. "No children," she wrote first. "Nothing but dirt. No grass or flowers grow here," she wrote next. Monica's paper was soon full of details. She was starting to <u>reclaim</u> her confidence. "I think I'm ready now," she said after a few minutes.

26   That night, Monica went back to the kitchen table. She wrote for a long time. She crossed things out. She put words in. Her hand moved across the page like a talented artist's paintbrush across a canvas. She hardly noticed when Ben threw soap bubbles on her. She kept focusing on the empty field. That field was her safety net.

27   The next day, Monica couldn't wait until it was time for poetry reading. When her teacher asked for volunteers, Monica's hand shot up in a flash. Her teacher called on someone else, though. Monica had to wait. In her head, she practiced reading her poem to the class. She thought about how her teacher was right. A poem can be written about anything—even an empty field.

Chapter 3

Vocabulary Development

This chapter presents information about the most common types of items used to assess vocabulary skills on state assessments. These include items to assess the use of context clues; knowledge of synonyms, antonyms, prefixes, suffixes, roots and base words, and multiple-meaning words; and the use of a thesaurus. The following are examples of reading standards for vocabulary development, not particular to any state. Students are expected to:

- use *context clues* to derive the meaning of unfamiliar words;
- demonstrate knowledge of *synonyms* and *antonyms*;
- apply knowledge of word parts such as *prefixes* and *suffixes*;
- use *root words* and *base words* to determine word meaning;
- recognize which meaning of a *multiple-meaning word* applies to the word's use in a context;
- use a *thesaurus* to locate related words.

Basic Strategies for Vocabulary Items

The following basic strategies are good starting points for teachers to share with students as they work together to make sense of reading test items about vocabulary. Later in this chapter, strategies that are specific to certain types of vocabulary items are explored.

✓ *Don't panic when encountering a vocabulary item that tests an unknown word.*

Encountering a word that students do not know is often the frightening part of a vocabulary item on an assessment. Even the most fearless readers can freeze when they come across a word they do not know on a test. What students need to know is that reading items that test vocabulary *intentionally* focus on words that are likely *unfamiliar* to them so that they can use their reading strategies to determine the meanings of unknown words. Therefore, students should be told explicitly that they are not expected to know the meanings of the vocabulary words—they are expected to figure out the meanings.

✓ *Recognize the item type and locate important information in the item.*

Savvy test takers pay attention to the directions and cues that are provided in items. For most vocabulary items, a word or phrase is selected from the passage and students are asked to uncover its meaning. Usually the item is presented in a straightforward manner, as in, "What does [tested word] mean in paragraph X?" Most state assessments set off the tested word in some way in the stem, such as by using underlining, boldface, or quotation marks. So that students can easily locate the tested word in the passage, the word is sometimes set off there as well; the main exception is passages that were previously published (because alterations of published texts are usually not permitted). Students might need practice with recognizing the kind of information in an item that is intended to be helpful to them in determining the correct answer.

✓ *Return to the passage and reread the targeted paragraph, not just the targeted sentence.*

Students will *not* have all the information they need in the item stem and answer choices for most types of vocabulary items; that is why a paragraph reference appears in most vocabulary items. Tell students to consider these paragraph references as big hints—and rereading is an important step to arriving at the correct answer!

Once students return to the passage, they should be sure to reread enough of the passage to help them gather the answer. Because many state assessments underline the tested word, students are tempted to reread only the sentence containing the tested word. But rarely does that sentence alone provide sufficient context clues for determining the meaning. Students should reread, at a minimum, the entire paragraph mentioned in the item stem in order to activate their thinking about the tested word's meaning.

When sufficient context clues are not found in the paragraph mentioned in the item stem, students should be reminded to expand their search for clues. Clues are not always found in such close proximity to the tested words as in the same sentence or the sentences immediately before or after. Sometimes clues can be found in the paragraphs before or after the paragraph in which the tested word appears.

✓ *Know the vocabulary terms.*

Sometimes "test talk" differs from "classroom talk," and that difference can get in the way of students' showing what they know. For instance, a test item might ask about synonyms, while a teacher and students might use the words *same meaning* or *similar meaning* to talk about synonyms in the classroom. To access certain vocabulary items, students must be taught to apply the terms that specifically appear in a state's curricular reading standards, such as *synonym, antonym, prefix, suffix, root* (or *base*), and *thesaurus*.

Context Clues

What does the word <u>suggestions</u> mean in paragraph 12?

A   Problems
B   Questions
C   Ideas
D   Reasons

Correct answer: C

Strategies

✓ *Locate important information in the item.*
The item stem tells students the following:

- What word is being tested (*suggestions*)
- Where the tested word is located (paragraph 12)

✓ *Return to the passage and reread the targeted paragraph, not just the targeted sentence.*
Students should reread paragraph 12 to search for context clues. If more clues are needed, they should expand their search to the paragraphs before and after paragraph 12.

✓ *Know a variety of context clues.*
Synonym clues are the easiest to detect, so students tend to favor this type of context clue. Students might need practice with recognizing and using other types of context clues, such as those in Figure 3.1.

In this item, descriptive clues are present, not synonym clues. In paragraph 12, Sara tries to help Monica by offering three tips: write about a family member, write about a place, or write about something she has read. These *suggestions* are *ideas* for what Monica can write about in her poem. By using these descriptive clues, students are likely to determine that option C is the correct answer.

✓ *Use substitution.*
Substitution is a popular strategy for vocabulary items probably because it is the easiest to use, but substitution should not be students' only strategy. Substitution as a sole or main strategy can lead students to believe that they need not look beyond the tested sentence for clues, and that one answer choice will make sense when substituted into the tested sentence while the three others will not.

In this item, because the tested word and the answer choices are the same part of speech, students can substitute the answer choices into the tested sentence easily:

A Sara tried to help with other <u>problems</u>.
B Sara tried to help with other <u>questions</u>.
C Sara tried to help with other <u>ideas</u>.
D Sara tried to help with other <u>reasons</u>.

FIGURE 3.1 **Types of Context Clues**

Synonym clue	When Juan finished the painting, he was <u>elated</u>. He was confident his art teacher would be *delighted* as well.
Antonym clue	Sandra knew she had to be more *careful*. Her <u>reckless</u> rollerblading yesterday ended with a badly scraped knee.
Example clue	While the musician loved playing *many types of music*, the <u>polka</u> was his least favorite.
Description clue	It was a <u>hazy</u> day. *Grey clouds crowded the sky and the air was moist. The sun refused to come out.*
Definition clue	The <u>flora</u>, or *plant life*, in China is interesting to study because there are thousands of species found nowhere else on Earth.
Cause-effect clue	The house was so <u>deteriorated</u> that the city was forced to *tear it down*.

Students should recognize that, stripped from the context of the story, all of these sentences make some sense. In other words, planting the answer choices in the tested sentence does not render three nonsense sentences and one that makes perfect sense. So, substitution alone will not lead students to the correct answer.

Students must combine the substitution strategy with their knowledge of the descriptive context clues they should have uncovered as they reread paragraph 12. Doing so will help them confirm that Sara is trying to provide Monica help with ideas—not problems, questions, or reasons. Option C is the correct answer.

Context Clues

Which words found in paragraph 1 help the reader know what <u>concentrated</u> means?

 A *had been sitting*
 B *had been thinking hard*
 C *sighed heavily*
 D *blank page*

Correct answer: B

Strategies

✓ *Recognize the item type.*

This item type is becoming more prevalent because it measures students' ability to select the words in the passage that serve as context clues rather than identify the meaning of the tested word. Students may need practice with this item type so that they readily recognize what is being asked.

✓ *Locate important information in the item.*

The item tells students the following:

- What word is being tested (*concentrated*)
- Where the tested word is located (paragraph 1)
- That the options are lifted directly from the passage (key words: *found in*; use of italics)

✓ *Return to the passage and reread the targeted paragraph, not just the targeted sentence.*

Because students are being asked to determine which actual words from the passage serve as context clues, rereading only the tested sentence won't get students very far. The only way to determine the answer is to reread the paragraph to find out if the words presented in the options contribute to the meaning of the word *concentrated*.

Furthermore, this item sets students up to think that only one context clue is present in the passage for the word *concentrated*—because there can be only one right answer to any item! But

there are context clues spread throughout paragraph 1. Students might find that the phrases *for more than an hour, come up with an idea,* and *thinking hard* all support the meaning of *concentrated*. By considering all of these clues, students will likely determine that option B is the answer.

✓ *Know a variety of context clues and construct try-out sentences, a form of substitution.*

As established in the previous sample item, synonym clues are the easiest for students to detect. But students need to know a variety of context clues (review Figure 3.1). In this item, students should identify the cause-effect context clue that lies within the structure of the tested sentence:

> *She thought if <u>she concentrated</u>,*
>   **cause**
> *she <u>would come up with an idea</u>.*
>   **effect**

In other words, *concentrating* has the potential to *cause* a person to come up with an idea.

Because students are asked to identify the clue that suggests the meaning of *concentrated*, they can construct "try-out sentences" by substituting the options into the tested sentence to determine if a cause-effect relationship exists:

 A She thought if <u>she was sitting</u>, she would come up with an idea.
 B She thought if <u>she thought hard</u>, she would come up with an idea.
 C She thought if <u>she sighed heavily</u>, she would come up with an idea.
 D She thought if <u>she had a blank page</u>, she would come up with an idea.

Placing the options in the context of the cause-effect sentence structure can help students think about which option makes the most sense. In this case, it makes sense that Monica thought if she thought hard about her assignment, she would eventually come up with an idea. Option B is the answer.

Synonyms

Which words found in paragraph 12 are synonyms?

A *funny, humorous*
B *think, tried*
C *place, read*
D *something, interested*

Correct answer: A

Strategies

✓ *Locate important information in the item.*
The item tells students the following:

- Where students should direct their attention (paragraph 12)
- That the options are from the passage (key words: *found in*; use of italics)
- That the correct answer is the pair of words that are synonyms (key word: *synonyms*)

Alternate versions of synonym items are presented in Figure 3.2.

✓ *Know the vocabulary term.*
In this item, students must know the meaning of the word *synonym*. If students do not make the connection that synonyms are words that have the same meaning, they will not know what they are being asked by the item.

FIGURE 3.2 **Alternate Versions of Synonym Items**

What is a synonym for the word <u>humorous</u> as it
  is used in the passage?
Which word has the same meaning as <u>humorous</u>
  in paragraph 12?
In paragraph 12, the word <u>humorous</u> has a
  similar meaning as the word _____.

✓ *Return to the passage and reread the targeted paragraph.*
Students might read this item and be tempted to select an answer without returning to the passage to reread, especially if the options present words they know well and two words stand out as synonyms.

Students should be taught that it is always a good idea to reread any paragraph that is referenced in the item stem, regardless of whether they think they already have a good hunch about the answer.

✓ *Use context clues.*
Rereading paragraph 12 and looking for context clues will likely help students determine that *funny* and *humorous* are synonyms. The context clues are that Sara has written about a *funny* aunt, and therefore she suggests that Monica write about a *humorous* person. Option A is the best answer.

✓ *Use substitution.*
Because synonyms are words that have similar meanings, synonyms should be interchangeable in the passage. Once students have a hunch about the correct answer, they can confirm their choice by replacing *funny* with *humorous* in the passage and vice versa. The original placement of these two words has been reversed in the example below:

"I'm writing about my aunt. She is so <u>humorous</u>," Sara said. That didn't help Monica. Monica couldn't think of any <u>funny</u> people she wanted to write about.

Students can also use this strategy to confirm that the other options are indeed incorrect. Notice that when students use the substitution strategy to try out option B, the passage does not make sense:

> *"I'm writing about my aunt. She is so funny,"* *Sara said. That didn't help Monica. Monica couldn't <u>tried</u> of any humorous people she wanted to write about. Sara <u>think</u> to help with other suggestions.*

Students can continue to use this strategy with the other options to see that only option A makes sense.

✔ Use knowledge of the parts of speech.

Students can use their knowledge of parts of speech to confirm their choice for the correct answer. Synonyms are often the same part of speech; that is, an adjective is often a synonym of an adjective, and a verb is often a synonym of a verb.

In option A, the words *funny* and *humorous* are both adjectives—and this is the correct answer.

While option B presents two verbs, the substitution strategy above shows that this option is incorrect.

In option C, *place* (noun) and *read* (verb) are not the same part of speech, nor are *something* (noun) and *interested* (verb) in option D. As students have likely determined from using other strategies, both C and D are incorrect.

Therefore, several strategies point to option A as the clear correct answer.

Antonyms

Which word is an antonym of <u>fail</u> in paragraph 2?

A   Miss
B   Choose
C   Explore
D   Succeed

Correct answer: D

Strategies

✓ *Locate important information in the item.*
The item stem tells students the following:

- What word is being tested (*fail*)
- Where the tested word is located (paragraph 2)
- That the correct answer is the antonym of the word *fail* (key word: *antonym*)

✓ *Know the vocabulary term.*
In this item, students must know the meaning of the word *antonym*. If students do not make the connection that an antonym is a word that has an opposite meaning of another, they will not know what they are being asked by the item.

✓ *Use prior knowledge.*
Because words often enter students' listening vocabularies before their reading vocabularies, students can draw on their experiences to place certain words in particular contexts. Students can ask themselves, "Have I heard this word before? Do I remember this word from something I've experienced or read?"

In this item, students will likely relate the word *fail* to the context of school and articulate its meaning as *to not do well*. Then students would know that the opposite of *to not do well* is *to do well*, or *succeed*, which is option D.

✓ *Construct try-out sentences, a form of substitution.*
To encourage students to consider all answer choices before selecting an answer, have them construct try-out sentences with the options. For antonym items, students need to add *not* to each option and place those words in the tested sentence:

A   "I'm going to <u>not miss</u> the third grade," she told her dad.
B   "I'm going to <u>not choose</u> the third grade," she told her dad.
C   "I'm going to <u>not explore</u> the third grade," she told her dad.
D   "I'm going to <u>not succeed in</u> the third grade," she told her dad.

Students should quickly recognize that option D makes the most sense.

✓ *Use context clues.*
Because the tested word appears early in the story, students can assume that the events and details that occur at the beginning serve as context clues. Students can put together that Monica clearly has a problem—she can't write a poem, her stomach is in knots, and she is about to cry. As a result, Monica thinks she will not do well on her big assignment. She will fail—or not succeed. Therefore, option D is the best choice.

Prefixes

In paragraph 25, the word <u>reclaim</u> means to—

A   happen without help
B   explain before
C   not notice
D   have again

Correct answer: D

Strategies

✓ *Locate important information in the item.*
The item stem tells students the following:

- What word is being tested (*reclaim*)
- Where the tested word is located (paragraph 25)

An alternate version of a prefix item is presented in Figure 3.3.

✓ *Look for familiar word parts.*
When answering vocabulary items, students should first look for word parts they recognize. In this item, students are expected to recognize that the segment *re-* acts as a prefix. (A list of prefixes commonly tested on elementary reading assessments is included in Section 4.)

FIGURE 3.3 **An Alternative Version of a Prefix Item**

Read this sentence from paragraph 25.

She was starting to <u>reclaim</u> her confidence.

What does the prefix <u>re-</u> do to the word <u>reclaim</u>?

A   The prefix <u>re-</u> changes the meaning to *without wanting to claim.*
B   The prefix <u>re-</u> changes the meaning to *claiming before.*
C   The prefix <u>re-</u> changes the meaning to *not claiming.*
D   The prefix <u>re-</u> changes the meaning to *claiming again.*

Students can make short work of this item just by knowing that *re-* means *again.* That's because only option D uses that meaning.

Caution students not to be thrown off just because they will likely recognize other prefix meanings in the answer choices. For instance, options A and C use the words *without* and *not*, and these are meanings for the prefixes *in-* or *un-* rather than *re-*.

✓ *Have an anchor example.*
Some students may quickly recognize that *re-* is a prefix, but they might not be able to recall the meaning that *re-* adds as a prefix in words. These students need an example word to *anchor* their understanding.

Teach students to think of other words they know that use the prefix *re-*. If, for instance, students are able to recall the words *reset* (for example, "I need to reset the video game player") or *review* (for example, "I need to review my notes before the test"), then they can figure out that *re-* means *do again.*

Sometimes students can find other words in the passage that begin with *re-*. Using context clues and their knowledge of words with the same prefix can further jog their memory about the meaning of the word part.

✓ *Construct try-out sentences, a form of substitution.*
To encourage students to consider all answer choices, have them construct try-out sentences. Because the options are phrasal definitions rather than single words, students must use their judgment about how best to substitute the answer choices:

A She was starting to <u>happen without help</u> her confidence.

B She was starting to <u>explain</u> her confidence <u>before</u>.

C She was starting to <u>not notice</u> her confidence.

D She was starting to <u>have</u> her confidence <u>again</u>.

Constructing try-out sentences helps students narrow the options by determining which make no sense—in this case, options A and B.

✓ *Use context clues.*

After constructing try-out sentences, students can consider their sentences within the context of the passage (to decide between options C and D, which make some sense on their own).

Students need only their knowledge of the events in paragraph 25, in which the tested word appears, to quickly determine the answer. In that paragraph, Monica finally has thoughts dancing in her head, so much so that she has trouble getting them all down; soon she is ready to go. Students can recognize that these details indicate Monica is feeling much better about having to write a poem and has her confidence again. Therefore, option D is correct.

Suffixes

In paragraph 14, the word <u>speechless</u> means—

A   without speaking
B   filled with thoughts
C   one who gives speeches
D   having more thoughts

Correct answer: A

Strategies

✔ *Locate important information in the item.*
The item stem tells students the following:

- What word is being tested (*speechless*)
- Where the tested word is located (paragraph 14)

Alternate versions of suffix items are presented in Figure 3.4.

✔ *Look for familiar word parts.*
In answering vocabulary items, students should first look for word parts they recognize. In this item, students are expected to recognize that the segment -*less* acts as a suffix. (A list of suffixes commonly tested on elementary reading assessments is included in Section 4.)

FIGURE 3.4 **Alternate Versions of Suffix Items**

In which word does –<u>less</u> mean the same as it does in the word speech<u>less</u>?

A Fearless
B Lesser
C Blessed
D Nonetheless

What is the suffix in the word <u>speechless</u>?

A ee
B ch
C le
D less

Students will quickly find the answer to this item simply if they know that -*less* means *without*. That's because only option A uses that meaning.

Caution students not to be thrown off just because they will likely recognize other suffix meanings in the answer choices. For instance, option B uses the words *filled with*, which represent the suffix -*ful*. Option C uses the words *one who*, which is a meaning found in the suffixes -*or* and -*ist*. Option D contains the words *having more*, which is a meaning for the suffix -*er*.

✔ *Have an anchor example.*
Some students may quickly recognize that -*less* is a suffix, but they might not be able to recall the meaning that -*less* adds as a suffix in words. These students need an example word to *anchor* their understanding.

Teach these students to think of other words they know that use the suffix -*less*. If, for instance, students are able to recall the words *fearless* (for example, "I am fearless on roller coasters") or *careless* (for example, "I broke the glass because I was being careless"), then they can figure out that -*less* means *without*.

Sometimes students can find other words in the passage that end in -*less*. Using context clues and their knowledge of these words with the same suffix can further jog their memory about the meaning of the word part.

✔ *Construct try-out sentences, a form of substitution.*
To encourage students to consider all answer choices, have them construct try-out sentences. Even though the options are phrases, the options fit into the tested sentence fairly easily:

A She sat <u>without speaking</u>.
B She sat <u>filled with thoughts</u>.

C She sat and is <u>one who gives speeches</u>.
D She sat <u>having more thoughts</u>.

Constructing try-out sentences helps students narrow the options by determining if any make no sense—option C in this example.

✓ *Use context clues.*

After constructing try-out sentences, students can consider their sentences within the context of the passage (to decide among A, B, and D, each of which makes some sense on its own).

Students need only their knowledge of the supporting sentences in paragraph 14, in which the tested word appears, to quickly determine the answer. In that paragraph, Monica holds up a blank sheet of paper—a detail that clearly tells readers that she still has no ideas for her poem. Monica is likely so frustrated that she cannot even respond to her dad's question. She sits without saying a word—*without speaking*—and instead holds up a blank sheet of paper as her answer to her dad's question. This information points to option A as the correct answer.

Roots and Base Words

> In paragraph 7, the root word in <u>guidance</u> means—
>
> A   to look for something
> B   to offer help
> C   to keep a secret
> D   to get easily
>
> Correct answer: B

Strategies

✓ *Locate important information in the item.*
The item stem tells students the following:

- What word is being tested (*guidance*)
- Where the tested word is located (paragraph 7)
- That the correct answer is the meaning of the root word in *guidance* (key words: *root word*)

✓ *Know the vocabulary term.*
In this item, students must know the meaning of the word *root*. Most assessments use the word *root* and expect students to know that a root word is the fundamental part of a word to which letters can be added before and after to form new words. Students might see the term *base word* used interchangeably with *root word* in various texts and instructional materials. Students should be taught that a root or base word is the main part of a word that gives it meaning—for example, *guide*—and that other word parts are what change the meaning—for example, *guid*ing, *guid*ed, *guid*ance.

✓ *Look for familiar word parts.*
In answering vocabulary items, students should be encouraged to look for word parts that they recognize first. In this item, students are expected to recognize that the segment *guid-* acts as a root. (A list of the most commonly tested root and base words on elementary reading assessments is included in Section 4.)

Notice how far students will get toward figuring out the correct answer just by segmenting the word into *guid-* and *-ance*. Even if students do not immediately recognize *guid-* as a root, they should be able to see that *-ance* is a suffix since it is found in familiar words such as *performance* and *appearance*. By identifying the suffix, all that remains is *guid-*, and therefore students might see that it is the root of a word that they know: *guide*.

✓ *Construct try-out sentences, a form of substitution.*
To encourage students to consider all answer choices, have them construct try-out sentences. Students can use substitution but will need to use their judgment about how best to insert the answer choices, because they are phrasal definitions rather than single words:

A She often liked to have her dad <u>look for something</u>.
B She often liked that her dad <u>offered help</u>.
C She often liked to have her dad <u>keep a secret</u>.
D She often liked that her dad <u>got easily</u>.

Constructing try-out sentences helps students narrow the options by determining which make no sense—options A and D.

✓ *Use context clues.*
After constructing try-out sentences, students can consider their sentences within the context of the passage (to decide between options B and C, each of which makes some sense on its own).

Students need only their knowledge of the supporting sentences in paragraphs 6–8 to quickly determine the answer. In these paragraphs, Monica thinks her dad will want to write the poem with her, but he walks away. Because Monica's dad often helps her (the passage refers to him as "her homework helper"), she is surprised when he doesn't step in; she decides she will have to turn to her brother for help. These paragraphs, then, offer clues that the root word *guide* has something to do with giving help. Context clues, then, help option B stand out as correct.

Multiple-Meaning Words

Read the dictionary entry below.

> **burst** [burst] *v.* 1. to explode or break apart
> 2. to be very full 3. to do something suddenly
> 4. to be very happy about something

Which definition best matches how the word
burst is used in paragraph 8?

    A   Definition 1
    B   Definition 2
    C   Definition 3
    D   Definition 4

Correct answer: C

Strategies

✓ *Recognize the item type.*

This item type is popular because it approximates the experience of a student looking up a word in the dictionary and negotiating each of its meanings. Students might need to be shown a sample of this item type so that they understand what is being asked.

Some state assessments present multiple-meaning words with definitions for at least two parts of speech. These items present students with a distinct advantage if they apply their knowledge of parts of speech; the answer choices that refer to parts of speech that are different from the tested word are not viable correct answers. Other state assessments present only those multiple-meaning words that have four meanings with the same part of speech; for these items, knowledge of parts of speech will not help students eliminate answer choices, so students must use other strategies.

✓ *Locate important information in the item.*

The item tells students the following:

- What word is being tested (*burst*)
- Where the tested word is located (paragraph 8)

- That the dictionary item is integral to negotiating the correct answer (key words: "read the dictionary entry below"; "best matches how the word burst is used")

An alternate version of a multiple-meaning item is presented in Figure 3.5.

✓ *Don't be enticed by the most familiar definition.*

Most multiple-meaning items present a *familiar* word to students to see if they can recognize a meaning for that word that might be *less familiar* or *unfamiliar* to them. That is, the purpose of presenting a multiple-meaning item is not to assess if students already know the most common use of that word; the goal is to determine if students can understand that a commonly used word has different meanings in different contexts.

For the word *burst*, students are probably more familiar with the definition *to explode* than *to do something suddenly*. Therefore, students should be mindful that they must look for the meaning that matches how the word is used in the passage, not

FIGURE 3.5 **An Alternate Version of a Multiple-Meaning Item**

Read this sentence from paragraph 8.

> *Seconds later, Monica* burst *into her older brother's room.*

In which sentence does the word burst have the same meaning that it does in the sentence above?

A   The pressure of the water caused the balloon to burst.
B   The suitcase burst with clothing and was too large to fit under the bed.
C   The football players burst through the large paper sign that said, "Go Team."
D   Her mother burst with pride when she saw her daughter on the theater's stage.

the definition that leaps out at them because it is familiar.

✓ Reread the targeted paragraph and use context clues to find a synonym for the tested word.

The structure of this item sets up students to read through four dictionary meanings before they read the actual question. Reading and thinking through the four dictionary meanings can be overwhelming, especially because the item does not provide the context in which the tested word is used. Therefore, students should be encouraged to return to the passage to reread the paragraph in which the tested word appears *before* they become encumbered by the four definitions.

Another good idea is for students to challenge themselves to think of a substitute for *burst* in the tested sentence. Doing so will help them begin thinking about which of the four definitions fits the context. For instance, in this item, students might choose *entered* as a synonym and substitute it: "Seconds later, Monica *entered* her older brother's room." Then students can read each of the dictionary meanings to find the one that most closely means *entered*. Option C is the best match.

✓ Construct try-out sentences with a key word from each dictionary entry.

Students can select a key word or phrase—a strong noun or verb, for instance—that sufficiently represents each dictionary entry. Then

they can construct try-out sentences to determine which makes the most sense. Students might need some practice with this strategy to understand how to insert the key word or phrase into the tested sentence.

The key words from the definitions that students might consider lifting are the following:

A *explode*
B *full*
C *suddenly*
D *happy*

The try-out sentences with those key words look like this:

A Seconds later, Monica <u>exploded into</u> her older brother's room.
B Seconds later, Monica <u>went full into</u> her older brother's room.
C Seconds later, Monica <u>went suddenly into</u> her older brother's room.
D Seconds later, Monica <u>went happily into</u> her older brother's room.

Students can easily eliminate options A and B. Because the sentences in options C and D make sense, students must depend on their knowledge of the context. Students who consider that Monica is actually quite upset because she cannot find anyone to help her with her poem will quickly eliminate option D. Therefore, option C becomes the only reasonable answer.

Use of a Thesaurus

Read this entry from a thesaurus.

bother *v.* 1. toss, shake
2. annoy, disturb
3. (Idiom) get under one's skin
4. (Ant.) help, please

bother *n.* 1. fuss, annoyance
2. irritation, difficulty, problem

Read this sentence from paragraph 10.

Monica should have known not to <u>bother</u> him while he was listening to his music.

Which word could be used to replace the word <u>bother</u> in this sentence?

A   Shake
B   Help
C   Problem
D   Disturb

Correct answer: D

Strategies

✓ *Recognize the item type.*

This item type is popular because it approximates the experience of locating a thesaurus entry and making a decision about a suitable synonym. For state assessments that present thesaurus items in this manner, students might need to be shown samples of passage-based thesaurus items so that they understand that they are being asked to find a suitable synonym for a word's use in context.

✓ *Locate important information in the item.*
The item tells students the following:

- What word is being tested (*bother*)
- Where the tested word is located (paragraph 10)
- That the thesaurus entry is integral to negotiating the correct answer (key words: *read this entry from a thesaurus*)

- That the correct answer is a synonym of the word *bother* (key words: *thesaurus* in the direction line and *could be used to replace* in the stem)

✓ *Use knowledge of the parts of speech.*

Because the thesaurus entry contains a lot of information, a good first step is to try to weed out information that is not viable. As it is written, the stimulus has six entries that students have to consider. Students should notice that four entries deal with the verb form of *bother* and two entries deal with the noun form of *bother*. Students who recognize that *bother* in the tested sentence is a verb can immediately eliminate the options that are taken from the two entries pertaining to the noun form. So, option C can be ruled out because it appears in the second entry of the noun form.

✓ *Recognize the need to identify a synonym.*

Because only the entries pertaining to the verb form of *bother* are viable, students can examine the four entries to rule out any that do not offer synonyms, because the item clearly asks for a replacement word for *bother*. Students need to recognize that a word that can replace another is a synonym.

Students who are familiar with thesaurus entries will determine that the fourth entry is not viable because the words following "(Ant.)" offer antonyms of *bother*, not synonyms. So, option B can be ruled out because it is an antonym of *bother*.

✓ *Use context clues.*

Because this thesaurus item is passage based, students can return to the passage to find clues for the meaning of the word *bother*. Students will likely key in on the words *snatched* (paragraph 9), *pitched* (paragraph 9), and *shooing her away* (paragraph 10) to know that Monica's brother is not pleased with her interruption.

With this knowledge of the context, students can now consider the options that remain (options A and D). Students will likely conclude that the first entry of the thesaurus provides synonyms for a different meaning of *bother* than how it is used in the tested sentence. The second entry, however, is a better fit—*annoy* and *disturb* describe how Monica's brother feels about Monica's request for help. Option D is a reasonable answer.

✓ *Use substitution.*

Because thesaurus entries offer synonyms and because synonyms are words that have similar meanings, synonyms should be interchangeable in the passage. Once students have a hunch that option D is the correct answer, they can confirm their choice by replacing *bother* with *disturb* in the passage:

D Monica should have known not to <u>disturb</u> him while he was listening to his music.

Students can further feel confident about their choice by substituting the other options to make sure they do not make sense:

A Monica should have known not to <u>shake</u> him while he was listening to his music.

B Monica should have known not to <u>help</u> him while he was listening to his music.

C Monica should have known not to <u>problem</u> him while he was listening to his music.

Using the substitution strategy, students can confirm that only option D makes sense and is clearly the answer.

Chapter 4

Important Ideas

This chapter presents information about the most common types of items that assess a basic comprehension of a text. For the purposes of grouping, their category is called "important ideas" and consists of the standards that pertain to main idea, details, summary, and graphic organizers. The following are examples, not particular to any state, of reading standards for the comprehension of important ideas. Students are expected to:

- determine a text's *main ideas*;
- recall or locate supporting *details*;
- *summarize* the major ideas of a text;
- use *graphic organizers* to represent or group ideas.

Basic Strategies for Items About Important Ideas

The following basic strategies are good starting points for teachers to share with students as they work together to make sense of reading test items about important ideas. Later in this chapter, strategies that are specific to certain types of these items are explored.

✓ *Recognize the item type, locate important information in the item, and know the terms.*

Main ideas. The stem of main idea items explicitly indicates to students what is being tested, usually with the terms *main idea, mainly about,* or *mostly about.* Stems also indicate if students are asked to identify the main idea of a single paragraph, a group of paragraphs, or the passage as a whole. A targeted paragraph(s) or sections of text will contain one clear major idea rather than competing major ideas; otherwise, there would be more than one correct answer.

Details. The words *according to the passage* are a signal to students that this item type assesses literal understandings—meaning, the answer is *literally* found in the passage. The answer might be stated exactly as it appears in the passage or the idea may be paraphrased. Usually detail items contain the words *according to the passage,* but other item types can use those words as well. Students should be taught that regardless of what the item is assessing, the answer can be found in the passage when the item stem uses the words *according to the passage* or *in the passage.*

Summary. Summary items usually include the term *summary* in the item stem. These items ask about the summary of an entire passage (especially in narrative passages) or a distinct section of a passage that can be summarized effectively (especially in informational passages).

Graphic organizers. Graphic organizers that are commonly tested on elementary reading assessments include outlines and lists, time lines, sequence charts, Venn diagrams, webs, and other diagrams, including the fishbone and the T-chart.

Most graphic organizers require students to read them in one of three ways: (1) from top to bottom, (2) from left to right, or (3) from inside to outside. (Occasionally, a series of steps are placed in a circular pattern.)

Other features of graphic organizers also provide clues for interpreting them. For instance, arrows and shading tell students how to direct their attention, and images that are either larger or smaller can give students hints about major or minor ideas or how ideas connect to one another.

Sometimes students expect graphic organizers to represent textual information in a particular sequence. Only those that clearly indicate a sequence need be in chronological order, such as sequence charts and time lines. Webs, on the other hand, are simply a collection of facts or ideas, so the information can be presented in any order.

✓ *Make the text more manageable with the "chunk, sum, and picture" strategy.*

Passages can be quite long, even on elementary assessments. When students encounter items for which they must return to the text to reread to find the answer, students can waste a lot of time and become overwhelmed merely by trying to locate where they should begin rereading! Sometimes students end up reading the entire passage again and again when they encounter several difficult items. The "chunk, sum, and picture" strategy can help students by inviting them to section off portions of the text even before they begin trying to answer items. This strategy is founded on a constructivist theory of learning (Vygotsky 1978), which suggests that students' comprehension increases when they actively construct their own interpretations of the texts they read.

Chunk. The sample passage "Searching for an Idea" has a problem-solution structure that can be divided nicely. For instance, the first chunk that should be obvious to readers is made up of paragraphs 1–7. In these paragraphs, Monica talks to her dad because she cannot write a poem. A second chunk can be made up of paragraphs 8–10, where Monica asks her brother for help. Paragraphs 11–12 can make up a third chunk; in these paragraphs, Monica calls her friend for help. By drawing a line across the page to section off the text in these chunks, students can reduce a long, overwhelming passage to more reasonable, manageable chunks.

Sum. As students decide on how paragraphs of text contribute to a chunk, they can identify those chunks with a short phrase to help them remember what happens. The short phrase serves as a brief summary, or "sum." As shown above, the sum of paragraphs 1–7 might be "Monica can't write poem"; the sum of paragraphs 8–10 might be "Monica asks brother"; the sum of paragraphs 11–12 might be "Monica asks Sara," and so forth.

Picture. Students can also react as readers by adding pictures next to chunks of paragraphs to further remind them of the major ideas—and sometimes just a "feeling face" is enough to capture the moment. For instance, students might draw an anxious face next to paragraphs 1–7 to express Monica's worry, or they might write "poem" with a large X across to help them remember that Monica is having trouble writing a poem. Next to paragraphs 8–10, a frustrated face might capture Monica's disappointment in her brother's lack of help. Next to paragraphs 11–12, students might draw a telephone to show that Monica calls her friend Sara for help. Certainly, next to paragraph 25, a happy face or a light bulb might express Monica's feeling when she discovers that she can write her poem about the empty field.

Using only one or any combination of these methods can make a passage easier to navigate.

Main Ideas

Paragraph 26 is mainly about—

A   how Monica works hard on her poem
B   what Monica decides to write about in her poem
C   how Monica's brother is playful with her
D   where Monica completes her homework

Correct answer: A

Strategies

✓ *Recognize the item type and locate important information in the item.*

The item tells students the following:

- Which paragraph is targeted (paragraph 26)
- That the correct answer is the main idea of the targeted paragraph (key words: *mainly about*)

Alternate versions of main idea items are presented in Figure 4.1.

✓ *Check your chunk, sum, and/or picture.*

Students who use the "chunk, sum, and picture" strategy (described at the beginning of this chapter) during and after reading the sample passage can return to paragraph 26 to see if their notes are helpful for this item. If, for instance, stu-

FIGURE 4.1 **Alternate Versions of Main Idea Items**

Which of these statements is the main idea of the passage?

What is the passage mostly about?

This passage is mostly telling about—

The section titled _____ is mostly about—

Paragraphs X through X tell the reader about—

What question does the last paragraph answer?

Which paragraphs in the passage would probably have this heading: _____ ?

dents wrote "Yeah!" and drew a smiley face next to paragraph 26, these notes might remind them that Monica is successfully writing a poem in paragraph 26. This notion matches option A.

✓ *Think big, not small.*

The correct answer to a main idea item "sounds" a certain way. A main idea is an essence, a gist, an idea that is so important that it is memorable. It is weighty. It is inextricably connected to one or more of the elements of a story—plot, character, conflict, resolution, and/or theme. It stands out. It is a big deal.

Details, on the other hand, don't hold the same weight in the story as a whole and don't connect to multiple elements of a story. For instance, when students see option D, "where Monica completes her homework," they should think, "Who cares?" or "So what!" Had Monica chosen to complete her homework outside, on a bus, at a zoo, or hanging upside down, it still wouldn't change the fact that she struggled to write a poem! Given what readers know about the plot and the information provided in paragraph 26, this option is not "big" enough to serve as a main idea; it is a minor detail.

By contrast, option A, "how Monica works hard on her poem," certainly is a major event that contributes to the solution or outcome of the story. The option also sounds like a big idea rather than a small one, especially given students' understandings of the plot.

✓ *Ask a critical question (or two).*

Students can ask themselves, "What is the one thing the author needs me to know about the information in this paragraph?," formulate their own response, and see which option it closely matches. For instance, students might say, "The author needs me to know that Monica is finally able to write her poem." Students might need to be reminded that the way they phrase their response will not always be similar to how the test does; nonetheless, they should be able to see the similarity between their response and option A, "how Monica works hard on her poem."

A version of that critical question is, for this item, "What would I not know if paragraph 26 wasn't there?" Students could read paragraph 25 and then jump to read paragraph 27. By doing so, they would realize that Monica hasn't written her poem yet in paragraph 25, but in paragraph 27, she is ready to read her poem to the class. Clearly paragraph 26 must tell readers that Monica finds a way to complete her poetry assignment, so this is the main idea. Option A captures that notion.

✓ *Look for evidence supporting the key words in the options.*

Students can pick out the key words that form the basis of each option. For instance, option A and B have similarities in terms of key words: *Monica* and *her poem*. The difference between

FIGURE 4.2 **Key Words and Supporting Sentences**

Key Words	Supporting Sentences
A works hard	She wrote for a long time. She crossed things out. She put words in. She hardly noticed when Ben threw soap bubbles on her. She kept focusing on the empty field.
B decides to write about	She kept focusing on the empty field.
C brother; playful	She hardly noticed when Ben threw soap bubbles on her.
D where completes homework	That night, Monica went back to the kitchen table.

option A and B lies in the words *works hard* in option A and *decides to write about* in option B.

After key words are identified, students can then determine how well the paragraph mounts information to support each option, as shown in Figure 4.2.

Option A shows that Monica puts in time ("wrote for a long time"), makes considerable efforts ("crossed things out" and "put words in"), and stays focused on her task ("hardly noticed" and "kept focusing").

Option B has little evidence, since the one supporting sentence is actually an extension of the information contained in paragraph 25, not paragraph 26. Students should pay close attention to the paragraph(s) referenced in the item stem; they should not be fooled by an option that presents an idea from a paragraph other than the one(s) targeted in the item stem.

Option C has little evidence, and this sentence actually supports the idea that Monica is focused on writing her poem rather than that Monica's brother is playful. Option C presents a minor detail, because paragraph 26 is certainly not "mainly about" Monica's brother.

Option D should be the least tempting option. It is an attractive choice only to students who believe in what might be called the "main idea item myth"—that the correct answer can be found in the first sentence of the targeted paragraph. Clearly, though, what Monica does is much more important than where she does it, so option D is a minor—not major—idea.

Looking for evidence to support the options' key words highlights that when only one sentence can be found (or stretched!) to support an option, it is likely because that option is a minor detail rather than an important idea. Multiple sentences can usually be found to support a main idea, which, in this case, is option A.

Details

According to the passage, why does Monica's dad ask her to go along to the grocery store?

A   He knows she will need more paper to finish her schoolwork.

B   He thinks they might find an idea for her poem on the way there.

C   He knows she is finished with all of her chores.

D   He thinks he might need her help with the groceries.

Correct answer: B

Strategies

✓ Recognize the item type.

The words *according to the passage* are a signal to students that this item is assessing literal understandings—meaning, the answer is likely addressed specifically in the passage rather than requiring an interpretation by the reader.

✓ Hunt and point.

To answer detail items, students should be encouraged to return to the passage to hunt down the answer, even if they think they recall the answer. Using the "chunk, sum, and picture" strategy described in the introduction to this chapter, students can use information in the item stem to know that they need to return to the part of the story in which Monica's dad invites Monica to go with him to the grocery store. Students should be able to recall that this event happens about midpoint in the story, and they can hunt down the information in paragraph 15: "We'll try to find an idea on the way to the grocery store." This sentence from the passage matches option B, "He thinks they might find an idea for her poem on the way there."

Students should be told that the wording of the correct answer may be literally lifted from the passage or may be a paraphrase of that same idea. Students should recognize that they can point to the sentence in paragraph 15 and to option B and realize that these are the same ideas expressed in different words.

✓ Hunt in vain for the wrong options.

For detail items—and items that use the phrase *according to the passage*—it makes sense that students can hunt for and point to the correct answer in the passage. Because there can be only one correct answer, students should also be able to read the three wrong options and *not* find anything they can point to in the passage to support those options.

As a way of confirming their choice for the correct answer, students should try to hunt for and point to any information in the passage that could support options A, C, or D. By working through each option, students should realize that they cannot find these ideas glossed in the passage. That is, there is no information that would lead the reader to think that Monica may need more paper (option A), that she has done her chores (option C), or that her dad needs her help with the groceries (option D). Therefore, option B is clearly correct.

Summary

Which of these is the best summary of the passage?

A When trying to do her assignment, Monica remembers that her teacher says a poem can be written about anything.

B After struggling and seeking help, Monica is finally able to write a poem.

C Monica's class has been reading poems, and now Monica has to write one.

D Although Monica sees many things on the way to the store, she doesn't know what to say about them in a poem.

Correct answer: B

Strategies

✓ *Recognize the item type.*

The word *summary* tells students that their ability to summarize is being assessed.

Another version of this item type is to ask students to supply a different title for the passage; for this item type, the words *another title* usually appear in the stem. This item type is categorized as assessing summary on some state assessments and as assessing main idea on others. The strategies suggested in this chapter for either standard should help students arrive at the correct answer for these items.

✓ *Check the chunks, sums, and pictures.*

The "chunk, sum, and picture" strategy (described at the beginning of this chapter) is ideal for helping students with summary items. By reflecting on how the passage can be divided into sensible chunks and rereading their summary notes, students are reminded of the overall direction of the passage and can use the information as a starting point for determining the best summary.

✓ *Put key pieces together.*

Because the sample passage is a narrative, students can think about the main literary elements to help them focus on the key pieces of the story:

SETTING + MAIN CHARACTER + PROBLEM + SOLUTION ATTEMPTS + SOLUTION = SUMMARY

Using this structure, students might respond in this way:

At home after school + Monica + can't write a poem + so she asks for help from her dad, brother, and friend + and finally her dad shows her an empty field and she writes about it = SUMMARY

By formulating their own response in this way, they can test their answer against the options presented in the item to look for the best match; students might need to be reminded that their response will likely be less concise than how the test presents a summary.

If students find a close match between their response and one of the options, they should still be encouraged to use other strategies to confirm their selection. If there is not a close match, the next strategy—a more item-specific strategy—should guide students to the correct answer.

✓ *Analyze each option for key words that relate to important literary elements.*

Students can analyze each option to detect key words that signify literary elements. Look at how each option can be labeled:

A When trying to do her assignment [problem], Monica [main character] remembers that her teacher says a poem can be written about anything [*minor detail*].

B After struggling [problem] and seeking help [attempts at solving problem], Monica [main character] is finally able to write a poem [solution/outcome].

C Monica's class has been reading poems [*minor detail*], and now Monica [main character] has to write one [problem].

D Although Monica [main character] sees many things on the way to the store [*minor detail*], she doesn't know what to say about them in a poem [problem].

By finding and labeling each significant part of an option, students can recognize that while all options focus on the main character and her problem and present the information from the passage, only option B avoids minor details in favor of including important literary elements, such as the attempted solutions and solution/outcome. The other three options tell half the story—less than half, actually! Option B is the most complete summary because it provides the fullest picture of the passage as a whole, and is therefore the correct answer.

Graphic Organizers

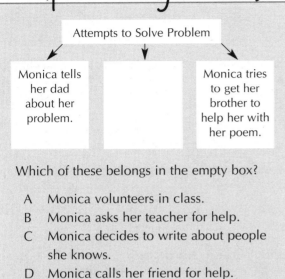

Which of these belongs in the empty box?

A   Monica volunteers in class.
B   Monica asks her teacher for help.
C   Monica decides to write about people she knows.
D   Monica calls her friend for help.

Correct answer: D

Strategies

✓ Be familiar with a variety of graphic organizers and how they are read.

In this graphic organizer, arrows indicate that all information connects to the box labeled "Attempts to Solve Problem."

Webs are simply a collection of information—facts, events, ideas, and so forth—and the information can be presented in any order. In this item, the missing information does *not* come *after* the first event presented and *before* the third event presented! Students can get tripped up by this random presentation of events; they need to be shown explicitly that the boxes would have needed to be connected with arrows showing a sequence (for example, from left to right) to require that the second box be filled in with information about an event that occurs between the events of the first and third boxes.

See Figure 4.3 for alternate versions of graphic organizer items.

✓ Use the "chunk, sum, and picture" strategy.

Because graphics usually capture significant aspects of the passage, students will likely have a hunch about the correct answer without needing to reread. In this item, for instance, because the majority of the passage is about Monica's problem and how she goes about trying to solve it, students will likely remember that Monica calls her friend Sara for help. Furthermore, students probably relate to Monica and her problem and have themselves sought help from classmates when in need; this plot event likely sticks out to readers and therefore is easy to detect as the correct answer.

Nevertheless, students can check a hunch against the passage using the "chunk, sum, and picture" strategy (described at the beginning of this chapter). Students can start by finding in the passage the location of the information provided in the graphic. Students might write the note "paragraphs 4–7" next to the box labeled "Monica tells her dad about her problem" and write "paragraphs 8–10" next to "Monica tries to get her brother to help her with the poem."

Then students should quickly be able to determine that the answer must lie somewhere after paragraph 10 but before paragraph 15, because paragraphs 15–25 tell readers about the solution to the problem. Students likely wrote something like, "calls her friend Sara" next to the paragraphs 11–12 chunk and can determine that option D captures this idea and describes an "attempt to solve the problem."

✓ Eliminate options that are not absolutely true.

Even if students have a hunch about the correct answer, they should check the other options against the passage to make sure they have good reasons for eliminating them. They can ask

FIGURE 4.3 **Alternate Versions of Graphic Organizer Items**

Some graphic organizers—such as outlines (a), time lines (b), and sequence charts (c)—pertain to chronology, so students must think about time order to answer the items.

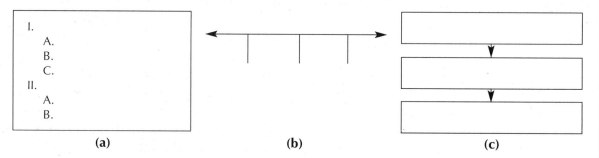

Other graphic organizers—such as webs (d), Venn diagrams (e), fishbones (f), and T-charts (g)—present a collection of ideas, so students usually do not have to consider time order to answer the items; instead, students have to think about the relationships among the ideas.

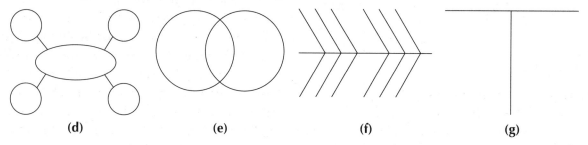

No matter the type, graphic organizer items usually ask students to add information, delete information, or summarize information, as shown in these three sample item stems:

   Which of these belongs on the blank line?
   Which of these does *not* belong?
   What is the best title for the diagram?

themselves, "Where did this happen?" and try to find evidence.

Some students may need help understanding that some options may initially seem true when, in fact, they are not. For instance, in option B, although Monica's teacher is mentioned in the passage, students have to determine that Monica doesn't directly ask her teacher for help. Instead, there are two occasions on which Monica *remembers* or *admits* that what her teacher has said is true: "A poem can be written about anything"

(paragraphs 17 and 27). Students should not be fooled by options that contain misrepresented information.

In option C, Monica's friend Sara does tell Monica to write about a person she knows, but no information in the passage indicates that Monica tries this approach. In fact, Monica dismisses the suggestion; she can't think of any funny people to write about. Later, Monica's paper is still blank, further illustrating that she does not try Sara's approach. Therefore, option C might at first have a ring of truth to it, but students who search for evidence to justify it should turn up nothing.

By eliminating options B and C because they are not true according to events in the passage, students are left with only two options to deal with.

✓ *Think connection, connection, connection.*

It is not enough for students to read the options to determine which of them makes a statement about the passage that is true. All graphic organizers are about the connections and relationships among ideas. Students can lose sight of this fact because graphic organizer items present a lot of ideas for them to juggle.

In this item, option A presents *true* information—Monica does volunteer in class—but this fact does not relate to the main topic of the graphic organizer, because it does not describe one of Monica's attempts to solve her problem. Therefore, option A can be eliminated.

Collectively, the strategies point to option D as the clear correct answer.

Chapter 5

Literary Elements

This chapter presents information about the most common types of items used to assess literary elements on state assessments. These include plot, character (including traits, motivations, relationships, conflicts, and changes), setting, problem/tension/conflict, solution/resolution, and theme/moral. The following are examples of reading standards for literary elements, not particular to any state. Students are expected to:

- recognize and analyze story *plot*;
- determine *characters' traits*, *motivations*, and *changes* by what the characters say and do and by how the author presents them;
- identify the *setting* and its importance to a text;
- recognize and analyze the story *problem* and *resolution*;
- determine the story *theme(s)*.

Basic Strategies for Literary Elements Items

The following basic strategies are good starting points for teachers to share with students as they work together to make sense of reading test items about literary elements. Later in this chapter, strategies that are specific to certain types of these literary elements items are explored.

✓ *Recognize the item type and know the literary elements.*

Plot. Plot items do not usually use the word *plot* or any other particular word in the stem to indicate to students that their knowledge of the plot is being assessed. However, plot items typically present one specific event in the stem, and the task is for students to connect it to another important plot event. Because plot items usually cover important aspects of the plot rather than minor events that are easily skipped over by a reader, the event posed in the stem should be relatively easy for students to locate in the passage. Usually the key to answering a plot item correctly is locating the event in the passage in order to make the necessary connection between the event in the item stem and the event in the correct answer.

Character. Items testing characterization come in many forms. On most state assessments, characterization can include traits (how a character feels or behaves), motivations (why a character behaves in a certain way), relationships (how a character reacts and responds to other characters), problems/conflicts (how a character faces challenges), and changes (how a character is changed or acts differently as a result of some event).

Character items usually include a key word in the item stem, such as *feels* or *changes*, to indicate to students which aspect of characterization is being assessed. The options of character items usually contain "feeling words," so students can identify the item type this way as well.

Character items do not usually ask about minor or flat characters. When minor characters are included in items, they are usually there to assess how those minor characters affect the main characters (in other words, character relationships).

Setting. The stems of setting items usually include the words *setting* or *takes place* to indicate to students that their ability to recognize setting is being assessed. Other setting items require students to go beyond simply identifying the setting. Such items ask about the importance of the setting to the story; in other words, students are required to consider how setting contributes to another important literary element, such as plot or problem. For instance, some problems in a story occur because characters find themselves in a certain setting; without that setting, there would not be a problem. Certainly these items require more analysis and are therefore more challenging.

Conflict. Items assessing conflict usually include either the word *problem* or *conflict* in the item stem. Some state assessments use the word *conflict* at the elementary levels, whereas some reserve the word *conflict* for middle and high school assessments.

Resolution. Some state assessments use the words *conflict, problem, solve, solution,* and *resolution* to assess students' knowledge of resolution, so students should be familiar with these terms. Students should also be taught to think about how a text's structure might give clues about the location of the answer.

For instance, in a narrative with a problem-solution text structure, the resolution is likely presented toward the end of the passage.

Theme. Some state assessments, especially for elementary grades, avoid using the word *theme* in an item stem and instead use the words *lesson* or *message* to convey the same notion. Students should know that any of these terms can be used in an item that assesses their knowledge of theme.

✓ *Use the "chunk, sum, and picture" strategy and text structure.*

Whether an event, feeling, or problem from the passage is used in the stem or the options, tracking down its location in the passage is always a good idea. These elements exist within a certain context, and it is important to have clarity about that context. Using the "chunk, sum, and picture" strategy, which is introduced and discussed at length in Chapter 4, students can access the parts of the passage that likely indicate or imply the answer to items about literary elements. Students who chunk, sum, and picture after their initial reading of a passage can go back to their notes as needed to answer various items. For instance, if a plot item asks about Monica's interaction with her brother, students can review chunks of text that mention him.

Students' knowledge of text structure also help them answer items about literary elements. For instance, students who have knowledge of a problem-solution structure of narratives can use what they know to access items about character, conflict, and resolution.

✓ *Look for connection and truth.*

Events or ideas that are used as options in literary elements items can be incorrect for a number of reasons. For instance, a true event from the story that is presented as an option can be incorrect because it doesn't relate to the idea posed in the stem. An example of this kind of incorrect option might be: "Monica's brother does not want to do his sister's chores [true event] because he is listening to music in his room [true event but does not relate to the idea in the stem]." Or, an event used as an option can be misrepresented (a little or a lot) and is therefore incorrect. For example, an item might read: "[stem] Monica tries to get her brother's help by offering . . . [option] to go to the store for him." Monica goes to the store, but not because she is going for her brother. These posers can be detected by returning to the passage to try to locate them. In the process of *not* finding them, students will likely uncover that the options are unrelated or misrepresented ideas, which invalidates them.

✓ *Think for yourself before letting the items cloud your thinking.*

Students who are able to make some sense of the passage before they encounter the items are often afforded a running start, especially for literary elements items. For instance, in a realistic fiction passage, students should expect to be asked questions about the main literary elements—plot, character, setting, problem, solution, and theme. Students who ask themselves the most basic of questions—"What is the passage about?"—are likely to home in on the important literary elements. A student might respond,

> *This girl has to write a poem for school but she can't. So she asks her brother but he won't help her. Her dad tells her to write about an empty field and she goes home that night and does it. She gets to read her poem the next day.*

With this basic understanding, students are well on their way to answering correctly many of the sample items in this chapter and others as well. So, savvy test takers take a few moments to reflect on their thinking about a passage before encountering the many ideas presented in the items.

Plot

Monica tries to get her brother's help by offering to—

A   go to the store for him
B   let him listen to her music
C   write a poem for him
D   do his chores

Correct answer: D

Strategies

✔ *Recognize the item type.*

Although the word *plot* does not usually appear in the stem, a plot item usually does refer to a specific event (for example, Monica tries to get her brother's help). Students can use this information to determine the section of the passage that will likely lead to the answer. In this item, students will need to locate information about Monica's attempt to get her brother's help.

✔ *Find the event in the passage.*

Because the answer to a plot item must be a true event in the passage, students should be able to return to the passage to track down the answer.

In this item, students should recognize that Monica's brother is a minor character that the author uses to add to Monica's frustration about her problem. Because the brother appears only twice in the passage—once in a significant way and once in a minor way—students should return to the passage to locate these instances. They should identify paragraphs 8–10 and paragraph 26 as the only mentions of Monica's brother.

Students should then be able to find the sentence in paragraph 8 that provides the answer: "'If you write it with me, I'll do your kitchen chores tonight.'" The students might also recognize that the reason Monica's brother throws soap bubbles on her in paragraph 26 is because he is doing his kitchen chores; he is having to do his chores

because he does not accept Monica's earlier offer to help her write a poem in exchange for her doing his chores. Therefore, both instances in which Monica's brother appears in the passage support option D as the correct answer.

✔ *Look for connection and truth.*

Plot items essentially ask students to determine which of four statements corresponds with the plot event mentioned in the stem. Therefore, for plot items to have rigor to them, the wrong options are usually details or events from the passage that have been twisted around a bit so that they do not relate to the event posed in the stem or are not quite accurate. In other words, instead of offering the option "Monica tries to get her brother's help by offering to *stand on her head*," which is a ridiculous option, the item poses that Monica agrees to go to the store for him (option A). This option takes a true event—that Monica goes to the store *with her dad*—and twists it around so that it is inaccurate—Monica does not offer to go to the store *for her brother*. Readers

FIGURE 5.1 **Options and Justification**

Monica tries to get her brother's help by offering to—	
Options	**Justification**
A go to the store for him	Does not happen. (Monica is asked by her *dad* to go to the store—she does not go for her *brother*.)
B let him listen to her music	Does not happen. (Monica's brother is listening to *his* music when she seeks his help.)
C write a poem for him	Does not happen. (*Monica* is the one who has to write a poem—not her *brother*.)
D do his chores	Does happen.

who are not paying close attention might choose this option because they remember reading that Monica goes to the store.

Students can write "does not happen" next to options if they can justify that an event has been presented inaccurately, as shown in Figure 5.1.

Using this strategy and the previous one, students can be certain that they have arrived at the correct answer, option D.

Character

In the passage, Monica's feelings change from—

A   confident to regretful
B   frustrated to satisfied
C   unhappy to puzzled
D   angry to nervous

Correct answer: B

Strategies

✓ *Recognize the item type.*

Two words in the stem, *feelings* and *change*, identify this item as assessing characterization.

This item looks more complicated than other types of character items. That is, many character items simply ask students to select one "feeling word" among four that describes a character. In this item, there are double that—eight feeling words! It doesn't seem logical, but this item type can sometimes be easier for students than character items that offer fewer words. If students can determine that one of the two feeling words does not adequately describe Monica, then the option can be eliminated. Students don't have that advantage with items that have only one-word choices.

Alternate versions of character items are presented in Figure 5.2.

FIGURE 5.2 **Alternate Versions of Character Items**

> Why does Monica change her attitude about _____?
>
> How does Monica change at the end of the story?
>
> How does Monica feel about _____?
>
> Unlike [another character], Monica is _____.
>
> When Monica finishes her assignment, she most likely feels _____.
>
> Monica's relationship with her brother is best described as _____.

✓ *Use knowledge of text structure and major plot events to question the options.*

Students can use their knowledge of the text structure (problem-solution) to think about how Monica feels when she is faced with the problem and how Monica feels as a result of having a solution, which logically signifies a change.

But all is not lost for students who do not recognize the problem-solution text structure. Students can think in terms of beginning, middle, and end in order to think about a change in Monica's feelings.

Students can use the basic question "When does Monica feel _____?" to help guide their thinking about the feeling words in the options. Then they can return to the passage to track down a major plot event to support the answers, as shown in Figure 5.3.

FIGURE 5.3 **Questioning the Options and Supporting the Options**

Questioning the Options	Supporting the Options
A When does Monica feel <u>confident</u>?	At the end; while writing her poem.
When does Monica feel <u>regretful</u>?	Never.
B When does Monica feel <u>frustrated</u>?	At the beginning; she cannot write a poem.
When does Monica feel <u>satisfied</u>?	At the end; she is able to write a poem.
C When does Monica feel <u>unhappy</u>?	At the beginning; she cannot write a poem.
When does Monica feel <u>puzzled</u>?	At the beginning; she cannot write a poem.
D When does Monica feel <u>angry</u>?	Maybe in the middle?; angry with her brother?
When does Monica feel <u>nervous</u>?	Maybe at the beginning?; she doesn't have an idea.

The answers to the questions in Figure 5.3 reveal immediately that option A contains a feeling word that does not describe Monica at all; therefore, option A cannot be correct.

Option B presents two feelings that describe Monica. Those feelings also present a change—from feeling frustrated to feeling satisfied. Those feelings occur at different parts of the passage—at the beginning and at the end. And those feelings fit with the passage structure—feeling frustrated about a problem and feeling satisfied as a result of a solution. Option B seems correct on many levels.

Option C presents two feelings that describe Monica, but these feelings occur at the same point in the story and do not show a change. That is, at the beginning, Monica feels both unhappy—because she cannot write her poem—and puzzled—because she cannot think of anything to write. Because these feeling words do not reflect a change in Monica, which is the task clearly posed in the item stem, this option cannot be correct.

Option D presents two feeling words—*angry* and *nervous*—that do not describe Monica at all. Monica is never clearly angry with anyone. And *if* Monica can be described as nervous, she is nervous at the beginning of the story because she does not have an idea for her poem. Still, there are no events that support a change in Monica from being angry to being nervous. Therefore, option D is definitely not viable.

Option B is revealed as the clear correct answer as a result of asking and answering questions about the two feelings (a strategy that can be also used for character items with one-word options).

Setting

The ending of the passage takes place—

A   at school
B   at a grocery store
C   on an empty field
D   at the kitchen table

Correct answer: A

Strategies

✓ Recognize the item type.

The words *takes place* indicate that this item tests knowledge of setting.

✓ Recognize how authors indicate settings.

Authors indicate settings with time (and changes in time) and descriptions of places (and changes in places).

The author makes explicit references to various settings throughout the passage. Students can track that information using the hints that the author provides, as shown in Figure 5.4.

✓ Pinpoint the appropriate setting that best answers the item.

Because the options in this item are settings that play some part in the story, students must pay attention to the words *the ending* in the stem and identify the setting that is featured prominently at the end of the story.

In this item, students have to recognize that the ending is actually the last paragraph, because that is where a change in setting occurs. Students also have to put together the detail that the assignment is "due tomorrow" from paragraph 4 in order to know that "the next day" in paragraph 27 places Monica at school. Other descriptive details are more straightforward and indicate that Monica is at school: "poetry reading," "her teacher," and "the class." Even though the author doesn't explicitly indicate that the last paragraph takes place at school, students can put together several pieces of information to recognize the setting. Therefore, option A is the correct answer.

FIGURE 5.4 **Tracking Settings**

Paragraph(s)	Settings	Evidence
1–7	Kitchen	"at the kitchen table"
8–10	Brother's room	"burst into her older brother's room"
11–15	Kitchen	"entered the kitchen"
16–17	In the car	"on the ride"
18–25	Empty field	"drove the car up to an empty field"
26	Kitchen	"went back to the kitchen table"
27	Classroom	"the next day"; "poetry reading"; "her teacher"; "the class"

Conflict

What is Monica's problem in the passage?

A   She does not think she can write a poem.

B   She does not get along with her brother.

C   She does not remember what her assignment is.

D   She does not want to do her chores.

Correct answer: A

Strategies

✓ *Recognize the item type.*

Students are expected to recognize the key word *problem* and associate it with the literary element *conflict*.

Alternate versions of conflict items are presented in Figure 5.5.

✓ *Weed out problems that aren't problems.*

For a conflict item to have rigor, students will encounter four options that appear to be realistic problems. For instance, in this item, not thinking you are capable of doing something you must do (option A), not getting along with a sibling (option B), not knowing what your school assignment is (option C), and not wanting to do your chores (option D) are all problems to which young readers might relate!

Because some aspect of all four problems appears in the passage, students might be lulled into thinking that each option sounds like more of a problem than it really is in the passage. For instance, in option B, "She does not get along with her brother" might have a surface-level truth to

FIGURE 5.5 **Alternate Versions of Conflict Items**

In the passage, what is Monica's main problem?

What trouble does Monica face in this passage?

What is the main conflict in this passage?

some readers because of the events in paragraph 10, in which Ben gives Monica no help. But Monica's efforts and actions in the story do not originate from her relationship with Ben. In other words, she does not call her friend because she is having a problem with her brother. She does not go to the grocery store with her father because she is having a problem with her brother. Monica's relationship with her brother is not her problem *in this story*.

Students can weed out the problems presented in the options that aren't real story problems by understanding that a story problem drives the plot. They should determine which problem best explains why Monica is sitting at the kitchen table feeling frustrated, why she is asking around for help, why she is going with her dad to the grocery store, and why she is excited to read her poem to the class the next day. In light of these major plot events, the main problem is that she does not think she can write a poem for school, which is option A.

✓ *Use the text type, structure, and title as clues.*

This passage is straightforward in type, structure, and content, and students can use these qualities to their advantage. That is, students will likely recognize that the passage is a narrative, that the events are presented chronologically, and that the content centers on a main character's problem and solution. Students likely know that in a typical narrative with a problem-solution pattern, the problem is usually presented early and the solution usually occurs near the end. In this passage, paragraphs 1–4 are the setup to the information provided in paragraph 5: "'I can't write a poem. It's too hard,' Monica said." Therefore, in this passage, the conflict is directly stated early on. Option A matches this idea.

Sometimes the title of a passage is also a hint about the problem/conflict. The title "Searching for an Idea" speaks to Monica's inability to find an idea for her poem—and without an idea, there can be no poem. So, the title is also best matched to the idea in option A.

✓ *Reason out the best answer of the four options presented.*

Students who read an item stem and immediately start formulating an answer in their minds sometimes get thrown off because the correct answer is worded differently than they expect. Many times this happens because the correct answer is worded in terms that are either "stronger" or "weaker" than how students want to phrase the answer.

Take, for instance, the correct answer, "She does not think she can write a poem." Some students might think that the phrasing of this problem does not capture Monica's conflict well enough; after all, readers are told in the first sentence that Monica has been trying for more than an hour. That's a long time to try to do anything without making any progress! Students might think to themselves that it's not just that Monica does not *think* she can write a poem, it's that she has tried and it appears that she *can't*!

Furthermore, students might articulate a different problem for Monica altogether. Because Monica tries to get help from three sources—her dad, her brother, and her friend—students might think that Monica's problem is that she is surrounded by unhelpful people! Students might think the correct answer should say, "No one will help Monica with her poem."

If students in a classroom discussion were asked about the conflict after reading this passage, they would likely have much more to say than "She does not think she can write a poem." But one of the limitations of a multiple-choice test, which must be addressed explicitly with students, is that test takers are searching for the best response among the choices, which does not always include the words that students themselves would use to respond to the question. Therefore, Monica's problem is that she is having a great deal of trouble writing a poem for a school assignment, and option A comes closest to capturing that notion.

Resolution

Which event helps Monica solve her problem?

A   She calls her friend Sara.
B   She tries to trade chores with her brother.
C   She goes on an errand with her dad.
D   She volunteers in class.

Correct answer: C

Strategies

✓ *Recognize the item type.*

The words *solve* and *problem* are clues that this item is about conflict resolution.

✓ *Find the options in the passage and use knowledge of text structure.*

Because the stem indicates that the options are based on events in the passage, students should locate and make note of where each option appears:

A   She calls her friend Sara.   (¶s 11–12)
B   She tries to trade chores with her brother.   (¶ 8)
C   She goes on an errand with her dad.   (¶s 16–25)
D   She volunteers in class.   (¶ 27)

Students can then draw on their knowledge of a problem-solution text structure: the problem usually appears at the beginning, attempts to solve the problem occur in the middle, and the resolution is presented at the end. Options A and B, then, are not likely the answers because those events occur toward the beginning, and the resolution of a story with a problem-solution structure usually appears toward the end. Furthermore, by locating option B in paragraph 8, students should see the event is stated inaccurately: Monica doesn't try to trade chores; she offers to do her brother's chores for him. A misrepresented event can never be the correct answer. Besides, doing or trading chores does not lead Monica to a solution.

So, tracking down the events and using knowledge of text structure help students determine that only options C and D are viable.

✓ *Add key words from the stem to each option.*

Because the item asks which event helps Monica solve her problem, students can add the words *and that helps Monica solve her problem* to each option. They can then use what they know about the plot to determine which is correct, as shown in Figure 5.6.

By linking the stem with the options as shown in Figure 5.6, students should be able to detect that option C is the correct answer.

FIGURE 5.6   **Adding Key Words and Using Knowledge of the Plot**

Add Key Words from Stem	Use Knowledge of Plot
A She calls her friend Sara (*and that helps Monica solve her problem*).	Incorrect. (Even though Sara tries to help, Monica still has nothing to write about after talking to Sara.)
B She tries to trade chores with her brother (*and that helps Monica solve her problem*).	Incorrect. (Monica and her brother do not trade chores, and doing chores has nothing to do with the solution.)
C She goes on an errand with her dad (*and that helps Monica solve her problem*).	Correct. (While on the errand, Monica's dad stops at an empty field—the place that is the inspiration for Monica's poem. So, going on the errand leads to the solution.)
D She volunteers in class (*and that helps Monica solve her problem*).	Incorrect. (Monica's problem is already solved when she volunteers in class.)

Theme

What is a theme of the passage?

A   Making a change in your life can be frightening at first.
B   Helping others is often rewarding.
C   Don't give up trying something that is hard for you.
D   Families teach us about ourselves.

Correct answer: C

Strategies

✓ *Recognize the item type.*

Students should recognize from the word *theme* that this item assesses their ability to uncover an important theme in the passage.

Alternate versions of theme items are presented in Figure 5.7.

✓ *Be familiar with themes.*

Often students need explicit instruction about what a theme of a story is and how the author helps readers arrive at that theme. A theme is the "take-away knowledge"—it is what the author wants the reader to take away from the reading experience, to turn over in the mind, to apply to one's own life experiences. Themes often "sound" a certain way—sometimes like good advice from one person to another.

FIGURE 5.7 **Alternate Versions of Theme Items**

What lesson does [main character] learn?

What message does the writer want readers to know?

What is most likely the author's message?

In this story, the main character learns a lesson about—

What is the moral of this story? (specifically for fables)

In theme items, students must decipher which theme fits the story from among several other themes. Students have to guard against being lulled into thinking that an answer choice is "close enough." All options will likely tempt students in some way (so as not to be far-fetched and easily dismissed), but only one option will be closely connected to the passage and therefore correct.

Figure 5.8 provides a short list of categories of themes as well as possibilities for how those themes might be worded on a state assessment.

FIGURE 5.8 **Common Themes and Examples**

Overcoming challenges	Facing challenges can teach you about yourself. Challenges can often be overcome with hard work and patience.
Facing fears and failure	Facing the unknown can teach us a great deal about ourselves. Everyone makes mistakes, so choose to learn from them.
Being an individual	Stand up for what you believe in. Find what your talent is and share it with others.
Change	Change is often difficult at first. Adjusting to something new takes time.
Being charitable	Giving to others is often the best reward. Share with others what you have.
Acceptance	Accept, don't judge, those around you. Accept what you have and make the most of it.
Friendships	Value your friendships. Friends can help you get through hard times.
Family	Families love you no matter what. Families teach us about ourselves and our lives.

✓ Focus on key words and ask key questions.

By focusing on key words in the options, students can begin to determine which theme is the most applicable to the passage as a whole:

A Making a <u>change</u> in your life can be <u>frightening at first</u>.
B <u>Helping others</u> is often <u>rewarding</u>.
C <u>Don't give up trying</u> something that is <u>hard</u> for you.
D <u>Families teach</u> us about ourselves.

Furthermore, because a theme of a narrative passage is usually related to the main character, students can formulate key questions about how the main character relates to the key words:

A Does Monica make a <u>change</u>? Is she <u>frightened at first</u>?
B Does Monica <u>help others</u>? Is the experience <u>rewarding</u>?
C Does Monica <u>not give up trying</u>? Is something <u>hard</u> for her?
D Does Monica's <u>family teach</u> her something?

By underlining key words and asking key questions, students should recognize that options A and B pale in comparison to option C—which captures both the problem (something was hard for Monica) and the solution (Monica does not give up) and is a "big idea" or the "take-away knowledge" that readers can learn from Monica's experience.

✓ Build a case.

To build a case for a theme is to collect events from the passage that specifically relate to it. This strategy helps students bring a discerning eye to each option; usually, students discover that there is far less evidence to support an answer choice than they might think.

For instance, option A, "Making a change in your life can be frightening at first," might seem reasonable if students associate or confuse Monica's frustration with "frightening" and relate the fact that she is finally able to write a poem with "a change." But if students build a case by looking for three pieces of evidence to support that theme, they will likely come up empty-handed. The same goes for option B.

Options C and D are different, though. In option C, Monica does face something *hard*, and in option D, *family* does comprise most of the other characters in the story. Students have to think through these more discerningly to uncover which of the two is correct.

FIGURE 5.9 **Building a Case for Options C and D**

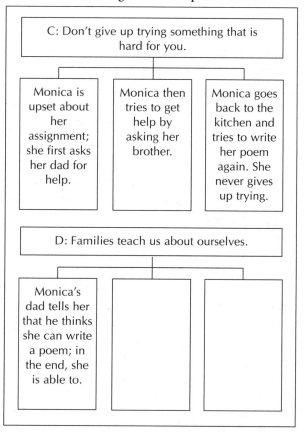

Students might need practice with a building a case, and doing so graphically can be critical to their understanding. Look at the supporting information for options C and D in Figure 5.9.

By collecting evidence, students should recognize that there are more plot events that relate to option C than option D. In fact, the evidence for option D is a bit of a stretch, because Monica never actually comes to realize that her dad has more confidence in her than she has in herself. Therefore, students can build a case only for the theme expressed in option C.

Chapter 6

Literary Techniques

This chapter presents information about the most common types of items used to assess literary techniques on state assessments. These include figurative language, simile, metaphor, hyperbole, personification, and alliteration. Because literary techniques are typically grouped within one standard, the following is an example of a literary techniques standard that is not particular to any state. Students are expected to:

> recognize and apply meaning to literary techniques such as *figurative language, simile, metaphor, hyperbole, personification,* and *alliteration,* in a variety of reading passages.

Basic Strategies for Literary Techniques Items

The following basic strategies are good starting points for teachers to share with students as they work together to make sense of reading test items about literary techniques. Later in this chapter, strategies that are specific to certain types of literary techniques items are explored.

✓ *Recognize the item type and locate important information in the item.*

The words, phrases, or sentences that compose literary techniques are not usually emphasized in a special way in the passages (such as through using underlining or quotation marks). Therefore, students should use the paragraph references provided in the item stem to return to the passage to find the example of the literary technique being tested. To stay focused on the example, students might choose to underline or circle it.

Some assessments approach literary techniques items in quite generic ways, such as by using the words *The author uses this phrase to mean____*. Other times, item stems specifically mention the literary technique being tested, as in *The author uses a metaphor in paragraph 26 to show____*. Students should be shown examples of item stems that are written in ways that both generically and specifically indicate that literary techniques are being assessed.

✓ *Know the literary techniques well.*

There are essentially two types of literary techniques items: those that ask students to identify the technique and those that ask students to interpret the meaning of the use.

It seems logical that identification items are easier than interpretive items, but the opposite can be true. If students cannot identify the literary technique as such, they have little hope of getting the item correct. On the other hand, students can often bring multiple strategies to interpretive items and have more of a chance of accessing the meaning of an example of a particular technique.

Therefore, in all cases, students who know well the literary techniques mentioned in the curriculum's reading standards are usually able to access both types of items. For most items, what constitutes knowing a technique well is being able to define the technique and bring meaning to an example of it. Therefore, students need many opportunities to identify and interpret literary techniques in various contexts during classroom reading and instruction.

✓ *Have anchor examples.*

In addition to being able to call up simple definitions of literary techniques, students can use examples to help them identify or interpret the literary techniques in items. Students should be taught how to extrapolate what they need from the anchor example. For instance, students who choose "Her voice is as annoying as fingernails on a chalkboard" as their anchor example of simile should recognize from the example that a simile is a comparison between two things that uses the word *as* (or *like*). By being able to refer to an anchor example, students have a better chance of accessing the information they need to answer an item about that literary technique. The activities in Section 4 allow students to explore and settle on their anchor examples of various literary techniques.

✓ *Use context.*

Students will *not* have all the information they need in the item stem and answer choices for literary techniques items that require interpretations; that is why a paragraph or section reference appears in these types of items. An item stem, for the sake of brevity, isolates the example of a literary technique, so it is important for students to return to the passage and reread enough of the surrounding text to understand the context. Often the context in which the literary technique "lives" is the best key to interpreting its meaning.

Figurative Language

In paragraph 2, the sentence "Monica felt a knot twist tightly in her stomach" means that she is—

A   strong
B   surprised
C   confused
D   worried

Correct answer: D

Strategies

✓ *Locate important information in the item.*
The item stem tells students the following:

- What sentence is being tested ("Monica felt a knot twist tightly in her stomach")
- Where the sentence is located in the passage (paragraph 2)

✓ *Recognize the item type.*
Students can have a difficult time recognizing figurative language items, other than in simile items in which the words *like* or *as* are specific clues. As a result, students need multiple exposures to figurative language items.

In this item, students must recognize that the lifted text ("Monica felt a knot twist tightly in her stomach") creates an image that is not meant literally—Monica does not actually have a knot in her stomach. Students then must figure out from the context what the interesting use of language means.

✓ *Get a general feel for the use of figurative language.*
Figurative language has either a positive or a negative feeling connected to it. For instance, the idioms *in hot water* and *stabbed in the back* convey negative meanings—and students can often figure this out without needing context clues.

Students should be encouraged, as a starting point, to decide if the use of figurative language being tested has a positive or negative meaning. In this item, students will likely determine that having a knot twisting in one's stomach would be quite uncomfortable—and therefore the meaning is negative. Because options A and B are feeling words that are typically associated with something positive—being strong physically is good and surprises are often enjoyable—these are not likely good choices for describing how Monica is feeling in paragraph 2.

✓ *Use context clues.*
Even if students have no conception of the figurative meaning in the tested sentence, they can use information in paragraph 2 to figure out the answer.

By rereading paragraph 2, students should recognize that the sentence before and after the tested sentence provide two clear clues: Monica thinks she will fail, and she is about to cry. These details direct students to option D, "worried." The other options—"strong," "surprised," and "confused"—cannot be supported by the clues provided in paragraph 2.

✓ *Use substitution.*
Students can use substitution to help them confirm their hunch about the correct answer. Each answer choice can be substituted for the figurative phrase:

A   "I'm going to fail the fourth grade," she told her dad. Monica felt <u>strong</u>. She was almost in tears now.

B   "I'm going to fail the fourth grade," she told her dad. Monica felt <u>surprised</u>. She was almost in tears now.

C   "I'm going to fail the fourth grade," she told her dad. Monica felt <u>confused</u>. She was almost in tears now.

D "I'm going to fail the fourth grade," she told her dad. Monica felt <u>worried</u>. She was almost in tears now.

This strategy helps students to see clearly that option A makes little sense; in fact, Monica is feeling quite the opposite of strong.

Options B and C don't make much sense either, given what students know about the plot. Monica is frustrated, but she is not surprised or confused about anything.

By reading the sentence that comes before and after the tested sentence and using substitution in this way, option D, "worried," stands out as correct.

✓ *Reason out the best answer of the four options presented.*

Sometimes students can be put off by the fact that their answer to the question does not directly match one of the four answer choices. For instance, if a teacher asked students how Monica is feeling in paragraph 2, they might respond, "Monica is *nervous* that she won't be able to do her assignment" or "Monica is *upset* that she doesn't have anything to write about."

Students should be taught not to be too concerned when their response differs from the correct answer choice; they should understand that their task is to choose the most reasonable option of the four presented. In this case, "nervous" and "upset" can be matched closely with option D, "worried."

Simile

In paragraph 26, the author uses the words "like a talented artist's paintbrush across a canvas" to show that Monica—

   A   daydreams about taking art classes
   B   is a better artist than a writer
   C   wants to add an illustration to her poem
   D   is creating something beautiful

Correct answer: D

Strategies

✓ *Locate important information in the item.*

The item stem tells students the following:

- What phrase is being tested ("like a talented artist's paintbrush across a canvas")
- Where the phrase is located in the passage (paragraph 26)

✓ *Recognize the item type.*

In this item stem, students are expected to notice the word *like* in order to recognize that a simile is being tested. Students are asked to interpret the meaning of a simile, rather than merely identifying the phrase as a simile.

✓ *Know common literary techniques well.*

By definition, a simile is a comparison between two or more things using the words *like* or *as*. Because only half of the simile is provided in the stem ("paintbrush across a canvas"), students must return to the passage to reread paragraph 26. Doing so allows students to locate "hand" in paragraph 26 as the other part of the comparison. Both parts of the simile are needed in order to derive the interpretive meaning intended by the author.

✓ *Have an anchor example.*

Students who see the word *like* and register the item as testing simile can use an anchor example of simile to their advantage. For instance, students who enjoy Deborah Wiles's book *Freedom Summer* might choose "I wiggle in my chair like a doodlebug" as an example of simile that they can stick in their minds. Then these students will be able to use it to recall that a simile is a comparison (wiggling in a chair is compared to how a doodlebug wiggles) that uses the word *like*.

✓ *Ask key questions.*

Once students recognize that their knowledge of a simile is being assessed, they can ask themselves two questions to focus on the comparison's meaning:

1. What is being compared?
2. What is the writer saying that these two things have in common?

As noted earlier, because the stem includes information about only one part of the comparison, students must return to the passage to hunt down the complete simile: "Her hand moved across the page like a talented artist's paintbrush across a canvas." Students must then isolate the two things being compared. Students might visualize that information as shown in Figure 6.1.

While simple, the graphic reminds students to ponder how Monica's hand moving across the page can be compared, or how it can be considered similar, to how a talented artist's paintbrush moves across a canvas. This is the right frame of mind as students consider each of the four options.

✓ *Build a case.*

As a result of being urged by the item stem to reread paragraph 26, students are likely to pick out details that relate to the comparison. They might focus on "crossed things out," "put words in," and "hardly noticed" to conclude that Monica

FIGURE 6.1 **The Comparison in the Simile**

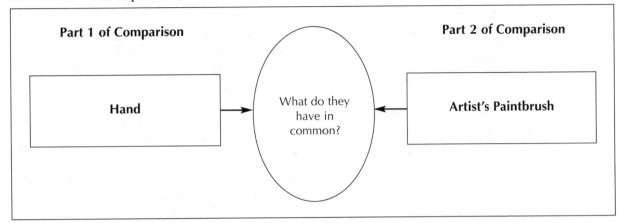

is focusing on her work intensely and that she is very skillfully putting together the words in her poem. These details are the support that is needed to make the case that option D is the correct answer.

But because the options are interpretive and "sound" like important ideas, students should try to build a case for the options as well; only then can they be certain that little evidence for the incorrect options can be accumulated.

For instance, students should be hard pressed to find information in the passage that supports option A, "daydreams about taking art classes." Although Monica tries and fails to complete her poem, it is not because she is daydreaming about something else—and certainly there is no information that supports the notion that she is interested in art. Therefore, no support can be found for this option.

Option B, "is a better artist than a writer," might cause students more pause than option A. Because Monica experiences a great deal of trouble with her assignment, students might be apt to think that Monica's best subject is not language

arts. However, no other detail in the passage mentions art nor does it reference any other subject in school, so students have no information to support this option. The author is certainly not making the comparison between how Monica writes her poem and how an artist paints in order to say that Monica is a better artist than a writer. That makes no sense.

If students are drawn to option C, it is likely because they are bringing in their personal experiences rather than relying on the information provided in the passage. That is, students are often asked, or choose, to illustrate their work in some way. So, students might be attracted to option C because it is a relatable experience. However, there is no mention in the passage that Monica needs or wants to add an illustration to her poem. And this notion has nothing to do with the question posed in the item stem—why the author uses a simile and what it shows. Option C, then, is incorrect.

Trying to build a case for each option reveals that only one option can be supported, option D, and is therefore the correct answer.

Metaphor

In paragraph 26, the metaphor "That field was her safety net" is used to show that—

A   seeing the field makes Monica not care about her troubles

B   Monica thinks she should write her poem about a safety net

C   writing about the field means that Monica can complete her assignment

D   Monica is reminded of a safety net when she sees the field

Correct answer: C

Strategies

✓ *Locate important information in the item.*
The item stem tells students the following:

- What sentence (metaphor) is being tested ("That field was her safety net")
- Where the sentence is located in the passage (paragraph 26)

✓ *Recognize the item type.*
In this item, students are explicitly told in the stem that the tested sentence is a metaphor. Therefore, students are expected to interpret the meaning of the metaphor.

✓ *Know common literary techniques well.*
Technically, metaphors come in many forms. Metaphors can be idioms, personification, and language use in which the intended meaning is metaphoric or figurative rather than literal. Often, though, state assessments test metaphor as a comparison stated directly (as opposed to a simile that uses the words *like* or *as*).

In this item, students are aided by the word *metaphor* in the stem. Students need to know common literary techniques well enough to understand that metaphors are direct compar-

isons. The stem points students to paragraph 26, in which the metaphor appears, because the context is important in deriving the interpretive meaning of the metaphor. Why a field is compared to a safety net is not immediately clear without consideration of other plot events.

✓ *Have an anchor example.*
Students who recognize this item as testing metaphor can use an anchor example of metaphor to their advantage. The activity on pages 202–203 allows students to create a memorable example of metaphor. Students who recall their example of metaphor (such as "I am a walking encyclopedia") can use it to recognize that a metaphor is a comparison (*I* is compared to an *encyclopedia*).

✓ *Ask key questions.*
Once students recall their knowledge of metaphor, they can ask themselves two questions to focus on the comparison's meaning:

1. What is being compared?
2. What is the writer saying that these two things have in common?

As noted earlier, students should return to the passage to find context clues that support the interpretive meaning of the metaphor. To do so, students must isolate the two things being compared. Students might visualize that information as shown in Figure 6.2.

While simple, the graphic reminds students to ponder how a field can be compared, or can be considered similar, to a safety net for Monica. Students should think of the qualities of a safety net in a literal sense in order to know why the author uses the image in a figurative way. Students might say that a safety net prevents someone from falling to the ground or it provides protection. This is the right frame of mind as students consider each of the four options.

FIGURE 6.1 **The Comparison in the Metaphor**

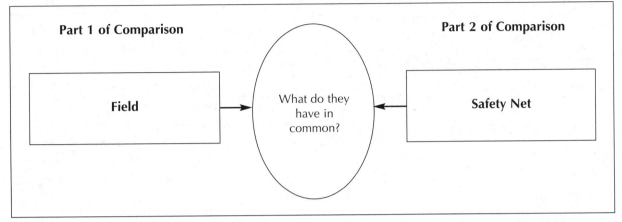

✓ *Build a case.*

As a result of being urged by the item stem to reread paragraph 26, students are likely to pick out details that relate to the comparison. They might focus on "crossed things out" and "put words in" to conclude that Monica is having success with writing her poem—finally! These details are the support that is needed to make the case that option C, "writing about the field means that Monica can complete her assignment," is the correct answer.

But because the options are interpretive and "sound" like important ideas, students should try to build a case for the other options as well; only then can they be certain that little evidence for the incorrect options can be accumulated.

Option A, "seeing the field makes Monica not care about her troubles," might have some appeal to students if they misinterpret what the option means. For instance, students might think that because Monica finds a topic for her poem—the field—she no longer has trouble. But that is a different notion than the idea that Monica forgets about her troubles. Students will have to think through this option carefully in order to eliminate it. Fortunately, there are no details that support the idea that Monica simply stops caring about needing to write a poem (which is what troubles her), so this option is not correct.

Students should be hard pressed to find information in the passage that supports option B, "Monica thinks she should write her poem about a safety net." Students might initially be drawn to this option because the words *safety net* appear in both the stem and this option. However, there is no literal mention of a safety net in the plot. It should be clear to students that Monica decides to write about an empty field and never strays from that topic. Therefore, there is no evidence to support that Monica writes about a safety net rather than the empty field.

Option D, "Monica is reminded of a safety net when she sees the field," seems as far-fetched as option B. When students recall the plot events that lead up to Monica's writing about the field, they will remember that Monica is initially confused about her dad's suggestion to write about the field. Monica says, "There's nothing happening here, Dad." The field doesn't remind Monica of anything at all. Certainly, the field, which is empty, does not remind Monica of a safety net, because if it did, Monica would have said that in paragraph 23. Therefore, no evidence in the passage supports the idea that Monica is reminded of a safety net when she sees the field.

Trying to build a case for each option reveals that only one option can be supported, option C, and is therefore the correct answer.

Hyperbole

Read this sentence from paragraph 2.

"I'm going to fail the fourth grade," she told her dad.

In this sentence, the author uses—

A   a metaphor
B   hyperbole
C   a simile
D   rhyme

Correct answer: B

Strategies

✓ *Recognize the item type.*

This item involves simple identification. Students need to use their knowledge of four literary techniques to determine which applies to an example from the passage. Of course, "simple" identification is not simple for students who do not know the techniques used as answer choices. Because they cannot use context or their understandings of the passage to help them, students who don't know the definition of hyperbole and cannot apply it will not be able to get this item correct, no matter how strategic they are as readers and test takers.

✓ *Know common literary techniques well.*

For items requiring identification, it is especially important that students can define various literary techniques. In this item, hyperbole is being assessed, so students should be able to define hyperbole as exaggeration (simply put). Students who know the definition of hyperbole will likely be able to apply it to the tested sentence.

✓ *Have an anchor example.*

Some students may quickly recognize how overly dramatic Monica is being when she says that she will fail the fourth grade because she is having trouble with one assignment. For these students, they'll recognize the answer as hyperbole.

But for students who do not immediately make the connection, they need anchor examples to help them distinguish which literary technique is correct. The activities on pages 198–203 and 205 present examples of metaphor, hyperbole, and simile that students can keep in mind. Other literary techniques, like rhyme, are probably so familiar to students that learning an anchor example is not necessary.

✓ *Ask a key question (or four).*

As stated above, simple identification items use well-known literary techniques as the answer options. Students must have knowledge of these literary techniques in order to answer the items. To help guide them as they weed out the options in this item, they can ask themselves a key question for each technique based on what they know about the definition:

A metaphor	Is there a direct comparison?
B hyperbole	Is there exaggeration?
C simile	Is there a comparison with *like* or *as*?
D rhyme	Do two or more words rhyme?

For option A, students could answer, "This is not metaphor because there is no comparison being made." Comparisons are made between nouns. In this sentence, none of the nouns (*I, the fourth grade, she, dad*) are being compared.

For option B, students could answer, "Yes, this is an exaggeration." Students should recognize that while Monica is frustrated, she knows that she will not fail the fourth grade because she cannot complete one assignment. Monica's frustration is causing her to exaggerate and be overly dramatic about the situation.

For option C, students could answer, "This is not a simile because there is no comparison being made using the words *like* or *as*." And again, the nouns in the sentence are not being compared.

Option D should not tempt many students, because students know that rhymes appear in poems and the text type is not a poem. Still, they could answer, "This is not rhyme because the author did not intend for these words to rhyme, and they do not."

So, knowledge of the literary techniques presented as answer choices in this item should clearly point students to option B as correct.

Personification

Which of these is an example of personification?

A   thoughts danced in her head
B   dad drove the car
C   she practiced reading
D   she had another thought

Correct answer: A

Strategies

✓ Recognize the item type.

This item involves simple identification, because students are asked to use their knowledge of personification to recognize an example from the passage. Of course, identification items are not simple for students who do not have sufficient knowledge of the technique being assessed. Even the most strategic test takers are stalled in items like these, because they cannot use context or their understandings of the passage to help them. Students who don't know the definition of personification do not have much of a chance of determining the answer.

✓ Know common literary techniques well.

For items requiring identification, being able to recall and apply basic definitions of various literary techniques is essential. In this item, students must know the definition of personification. Students need to be taught explicitly that personification is giving human qualities to nonhuman things.

✓ Have an anchor example.

Students who recognize this item as testing personification will be able to make good use of an anchor example of personification. The activity on pages 203–204 allows students to create a memorable example (such as *The stars refused to show up for work last night*) so that they can recall and use this anchor to help them during a reading assessment.

✓ Find the noun and find the verb.

In this item, the options are actual phrases lifted from the passage. Because personification hinges on giving human qualities (usually a verb) to nonhuman things (usually a noun or the subject), it is rare for personification to exist without a noun and a verb. (Occasionally, personification can be created with an adjective and a noun, as in *whispering wind*, but these examples are more infrequent in literature than a noun-verb combination.)

Students should develop some kind of marking system to focus their attention on the noun and the verb in each option, as illustrated below, where the nouns are put into parentheses and the verbs are underlined:

A   (thoughts) <u>danced</u> in her head
B   (dad) <u>drove</u> the car
C   (she) <u>practiced</u> reading
D   (she) <u>had</u> another thought

By isolating the nouns and verbs in the options, students can begin to rule out the options that do not fit the definition of personification—ascribing something nonhuman (noun) to something human (verb).

Additionally, advise students that if, in a few cases, the isolation of the subject and the verb fails to reveal an example of personification, they should isolate the subject (which will be the nonhuman thing) and look for other parts of speech that indicate a human quality, such as adjectives (for example, *The angry sun*).

✓ Find something human and nonhuman.

Working with the identification of nouns/subjects and verbs in the options, students can then pose questions about whether the noun/subject refers to something nonhuman and the verb to something human:

A Are (thoughts) nonhuman? Do humans <u>dance</u>?

B Is a (dad) nonhuman? Do humans <u>drive</u>?

C Is (she) nonhuman? Is <u>practiced</u> human?

D Is (she) nonhuman? Is <u>had</u> human?

Clearly options B, C, and D make no sense because the noun *dad* and the pronoun *she* refer to humans. The first question alone eliminates these options as viable.

That leaves option A. Are thoughts nonhuman? Yes, thoughts are abstract things—not living, breathing, functioning humans. Do humans dance? Yes, humans dance—sometimes badly, but still, they try.

✓ *Ask a key question.*

Because personification, by definition, is attributing a human quality to a nonhuman or abstract thing, personification has a figurative meaning, not a literal one.

Students can check their answer by making sure the example is not literal in meaning. They can ask themselves, "Did that *actually* happen?" Students should immediately recognize that, for option A, thoughts didn't *actually* dance in Monica's head.

Students can also check to make sure that the options they eliminated are indeed wrong. They can ask, "Did Monica's dad *actually* drive?," "Did Monica *actually* practice reading?," and "Did Monica *actually* have another thought?" Because the answer is yes to these questions, options B, C, and D cannot be examples of personification.

Alliteration

Read this sentence from paragraph 22.

Monica sat still and stared ahead, pondering why her dad wanted her to look at the empty field.

Which words are an example of alliteration?

A   *sat still and stared*
B   *pondering why*
C   *wanted her to look*
D   *at the empty field*

Correct answer: A

Strategies

✓ *Recognize the item type.*

This item involves simple identification. Students need to apply their knowledge of the alliteration to an example from the passage. Of course, the item will not be simple for students who cannot drum up the definition of *alliteration*. This item is like an "isolated" or "stand-alone" item (typically defined as a reading item that is not connected to a passage), because students cannot use context or their understandings of the passage to help them. No matter how strategic they are as readers and test takers, students who do not bring knowledge of alliteration to the table will not likely answer this item correctly.

Some state assessments include alliteration items only with poetry. Other assessments test alliteration in various types of texts as well as in isolation. In this item, students are explicitly directed to search for alliteration in a particular sentence. Other items might ask students to analyze a particular phrase or sentence and identify it as alliteration, among other techniques as options.

✓ *Know common literary techniques well.*

By definition, alliteration is the repetition of the initial sound in two or more words. Students are often highly capable of recognizing alliteration, perhaps more so than other literary techniques, because of repeated exposure to examples early on in their education. Some students have an easy time of identifying alliteration in items like these, especially if they use the strategies that follow.

✓ *Have an anchor example.*

Students who recognize this item as testing alliteration can call on an anchor example to find the correct answer. For instance, students who enjoy the book *Some Smug Slug* by Pamela Duncan Edwards might recall that the title itself is an example of alliteration. The activity on pages 206–207 also reinforces the definition of alliteration and provides opportunities for students to create their own memorable examples.

✓ *Underline, underline, underline.*

One technique for drawing attention to alliteration is to ask students to underline the first letter of each word in a targeted phrase or sentence:

Monica sat still and stared ahead, pondering why her dad wanted her to look at the empty field.

Doing so reminds them that alliteration hinges on the initial sounds of words, so examples of alliteration essentially reveal themselves to students.

Students should recognize that *sat* and *still* are words that have the same beginning letter and are side by side in the targeted sentence. When they look for those words in the options, they will see that option A, "sat still and stared," is correct.

An even better strategy, especially on timed assessments, is for students to shortcut this strategy by underlining the initial letter of each word in the options:

A *sat still and stared*
B *pondering why*
C *wanted her to look*
D *at the empty field*

Because only option A contains words that begin with the same letter, it is the correct answer.

Chapter 7

Interpretations

This chapter presents information about the most common types of items used to assess interpretations on state assessments—those which typically require critical thinking. These include cause-effect, chronology, conclusion/inference, fact/opinion, prediction, and supporting evidence. The following are examples, not particular to any state, of reading standards for interpretations. Students are expected to:

- recognize a cause for an effect and an effect for a cause in stated and inferred *cause-effect relationships*;
- place events in *chronological* (time order) sequence;
- use evidence from the passage to draw a *conclusion* or make an *inference*;
- distinguish *fact* from *opinion*;
- make a reasonable *prediction* based on information in the passage;
- *support* an assertion or conclusion with *evidence* from the passage.

Basic Strategies for Interpretation Items

The following basic strategies are good starting points for teachers to share with students as they work together to make sense of reading test items about interpretations. Later in this chapter, strategies that are specific to certain types of interpretation items are explored.

✓ *Recognize the item type.*

Cause-effect. There is usually at least one recognizable clue in the stem of an item testing cause-effect. The words *cause, effect, why, because, result,* or *outcome* in the stem tell students to think about a relationship between two events.

The distractors for a cause-effect item can be true events from the passage or they can be misrepresented events; either way, the distractors will be wrong because they do not have a direct connection to the event specified in the item stem.

Chronology. There is usually at least one recognizable clue in the stem of an item testing chronology. The phrases *which event occurs* or *what happens* indicate to students that they should think about text chronology, as do the words *before, after, first,* and *last.*

Typically, the options for a chronology item will be true events from the passage, accurately represented. Students do not have the advantage of trying to determine if any option does not appear in the passage and is therefore not viable. So, students really have to home in on the relationship that is being established between the event featured in the stem and the one correct answer.

Conclusion/inference. Conclusion/inference items test students' ability to take what the author tells them explicitly and draw reasonable conclusions or make reasonable inferences about that information. Such items require high-level thinking and can be difficult for students. The phrase *based on* and words such as *tell, conclude,* and *infer* are signals to students that they cannot simply point to these exact words in the passage that appear in the answer.

Prediction. While there are a number of ways to phrase prediction items, students are provided with clue words in the stems to indicate that the items test prediction; otherwise, students will not know that they have to think beyond the boundaries of the passage. These clue words include *will happen next, after the story ends, the reader can predict that, if the story had continued,* and *in the future.*

Fact/Opinion. Identifying items that test opinions is easy for students because the word *opinion* will appear in the stems. For items testing facts, the word *fact* will appear. Usually, there is no variation on the phrasing of fact/opinion items.

Supporting Evidence. The structure of supporting evidence items is usually the same: Students are provided with a conclusion or an important idea in the stem, such as a character trait or theme, and are asked to select from among four quoted sentences or four paraphrased ideas the information that best supports the idea presented in the stem. The quoted text can come from one paragraph or from various paragraphs. The options might be ordered according to how they appear in the passage or they may be scrambled. The options might or might not be set off in a special way—such as with italics—to indicate that they are lifted from the passage.

✓ *Locate the options in the passage.*

For items that assess *literal* understandings, such as those testing details, it makes perfect sense to track down the options in the passage in order to be able to point to the answer—after all, the answer is often stated *literally* in the passage.

But it's also important to track down the options in the passage for other types of items—even those requiring *interpretations*. The options for many types of interpretation items are true events (or true information) from the passage. So, simply knowing where the events (that the options describe) appear in the passage can offer clues about the answers to various interpretation items. Take cause-effect relationships, for instance. In the typical structure of a text, usually a cause precedes an effect; the author presents a cause and effect in close proximity so that readers will recognize that a relationship exists. Therefore, students who track down the events in the item stem and options and find that two exist reasonably close together are provided with a hint that a cause-effect relationship might exist between them.

As another example, chronology items ask students to juggle *five* events at once—the event provided in the item stem and the event presented in each of the four options. In order to keep the events from muddling in their minds, students should take a moment to find each event in the passage and make note of it. Often the answer to a chronology item reveals itself to students while they are in the process of tracking down the options. If not, students can use other clues—such as settings—to make sense of which events precede or follow others.

Encouraging students to return to the passage to track down events and important information—even with items that require interpretations—can build their understanding that the answers to items lie somewhere within the text itself, sometimes literally stated and sometimes bubbling just beneath the surface.

✓ *Ask a key question.*

Readers might have noticed that "ask a key question" is a strategy that has been sprinkled into previous chapters for certain types of items. In essence, this strategy in its many forms helps students get to the heart of certain definitions and features that compose certain types of items. Some of the key questions students can ask themselves for the standards in this chapter are shown in Figure 7.1.

Posing questions in this way requires students to think about the core of a particular reading standard. In many ways, key questions set students on the necessary path toward determining the correct answer.

FIGURE 7.1
**Item Types and
Key Questions**

Item Types	Key Questions
Cause-effect	Does [this] lead to [that]? or Did [that] cause [this]?
Chronology	Does [this] precede/follow [that]?
Conclusion/Inference	What does the passage say about [this]?
Prediction	Can readers know [this]?

✓ *Build a case.*

Readers might also have noticed that "build a case" is a strategy that has been sprinkled into previous chapters for certain types of items. If the strategy's name sounds a bit like something a lawyer would do, that's the intent. Building a case for the options of an item is a strategy that asks students to think through each one and to formulate reasons and find evidence that make an option either correct or incorrect. While building a case is another way of saying "support the answer" and can be applied to many types of items, the strategy is especially helpful to use with items about interpretations. Students have come to think of these as "brain questions," thanks to Taffy E. Raphael's (1982) QAR (Question-Answer-Relationships) model. Simply put, brain questions are those for which students must use their brains to put information together to support an answer rather than locate the answer stated on the test page. For many item types in this chapter, students can learn to arrive at the correct answer by attempting to build a case for each option as either well-supported or not supported at all.

Cause-Effect

Monica is able to find a subject for her poem because—

A   she remembers what her teacher tells her
B   her dad takes her on an errand
C   her brother writes a poem for her
D   she wants to read a poem to her class

Correct answer: B

Strategies

✓ *Recognize the item type.*

The word *because* tells students that they should think about a cause-effect relationship.

The options for this cause-effect item are true events from the passage, so students must determine which three are wrong because they do not have a direct relationship to the event specified in the item stem.

Alternate versions of cause-effect items are presented in Figure 7.2.

✓ *Figure out which part of the cause-effect relationship is provided.*

In a cause-effect relationship item, the cause can be provided and students must recognize the effect, or the effect can be provided and students

FIGURE 7.2 **Alternate Versions of Cause-Effect Items**

Monica is able to find a subject for her poem
  because—
What *causes* Monica to find a subject for her poem?
Why is Monica able to find a subject for her poem?
What is the *effect* of Monica going on an errand with her dad?
As a result of going on an errand with her dad, Monica—
What is an important *outcome* of Monica going on an errand with her dad?

FIGURE 7.3 **Visualizing a Cause-Effect Relationship**

Cause	➔	Effect
?	LEADS TO	Monica is able to find a subject for her poem.

must recognize the cause. When the stem does not use the words *cause* or *effect*, it might be difficult initially for students to understand which part of a cause-effect relationship they are searching for. Students can use the key word *because* to know that they are looking for the cause and that the stem provides the effect. Visualizing the relationship in graphic form, as shown in Figure 7.3, can help.

✓ *Ask a key question.*

Sometimes when a cause-effect item provides the effect in the stem and asks for the cause, as is the case with this item, students can become confused because the information feels "backward." Posing the relationship as a question can help test the sense of each option:

A Does *remembering what her teacher tells her* **cause** Monica to find a subject for her poem?
B Does *her dad's taking her on an errand* **cause** Monica to find a subject for her poem?
C Does *her brother's writing a poem for her* **cause** Monica to find a subject for her poem?
D Does *wanting to read a poem to her class* **cause** Monica to find a subject for her poem?

Option B represents the direct relationship that occurs in the story—only because Monica goes on an errand with her dad is she taken to the empty field that becomes the subject of her poem. A clear relationship does not exist in the other options. In option A, remembering what her teacher tells her ("You can write about anything") does not give Monica a subject for her poem. In option C, her brother's poem is a joke—he doesn't make a serious attempt to help her—and it certainly does not give Monica a subject to write about. In option D, wanting to read a poem to her class makes little sense because Monica cannot read her poem if she has not written one! Therefore, students can use their constructed questions to determine that a clear cause-effect relationship is made with option B.

✔ *Locate the events in the stem and the options in the passage.*

Sometimes the structure of events in the passage can be a clue about the cause-effect relationship. In a narrative story in which the events are chronological, as in the passage "Searching for an Idea," an effect usually comes after a cause. (Students might need to explore an exception to this strategy: In an informational passage—especially a newspaper article—the effect might be told in the first paragraph and the remainder of the article might describe the causes that led to that effect.)

By locating the events in the passage and writing the paragraph reference next to the stem and each option, students can find which event precedes the one provided in the stem:

Effect: Monica is able to find a subject
for her poem because—   (¶s 25–26)
A she remembers what her teacher
   tells her   (¶ 17)
B her dad takes her on an errand (¶s 15–24)
C her brother writes a poem for her (¶s 8–10)
D she wants to read a poem to her
   class   (¶ 27)

Option B appears to be the most viable answer because it appears in paragraphs 15–24, and the item stem, which provides the effect, appears in paragraphs 25–26. The other options either appear a great distance away from the effect provided in the stem (options A and C) or *after* the effect provided in the stem (option D), and therefore are less viable because they do not fit the usual cause-effect structure.

Chronology

What happens right after Dad tells Monica that she should write about the empty field?

A　Monica makes notes about what she sees.
B　Monica practices her poem in her head.
C　Monica's brother throws soap bubbles on her.
D　Monica remembers her teacher's advice.

Correct answer: A

Strategies

✓ *Recognize the item type.*

The phrase "What happens right after" tells students that they should think about the text's chronology.

Alternate versions of chronology items are presented in Figure 7.4.

✓ *Locate the events in the stem and the options in the passage.*

Returning to the passage to locate the events and putting a paragraph reference next to each option reminds students about the plot's chronology:

What happens right after Dad tells Monica
  that she should write about the empty
  field?　　　　　　　　　(¶s 19–24)
A Monica makes notes about what
  she sees.　　　　　　　　(¶ 25)
B Monica practices her poem in her
  head.　　　　　　　　　(¶ 27)
C Monica's brother throws soap bubbles
  on her.　　　　　　　　(¶ 26)
D Monica remembers her teacher's
  advice.　　　　　　　　(¶ 17)

The paragraph references help students think through whether option A, which appears in paragraph 25, really does list an event that comes right after the event in the stem, which appears in paragraphs 19–24.

FIGURE 7.4　**Alternate Versions of Chronology Items**

> Which event happened *first* in the story?
> Which of these events happened *last*?
> What must happen *before* _____?
> *When* _____ goes to do _____, what happens?
> What happens *right after* _____?

Students can then use any of the strategies below to think about the time order of the events rather than simply their location in the passage.

✓ *Use a graphic organizer to think about time order.*

Putting the events on a time line or in sequenced boxes helps students to think about chronology. After students make note of paragraph references for each option, they can confirm whether the plot makes sense if the events are ordered according to where they appear in the passage, as shown in Figure 7.5.

By using a time line, students can see that option D does not belong on the time line because it is an event that comes *before* the event provided in the stem rather than "right after."

Because a chronology item isn't simply asking where the event appears in the passage, but rather when the event occurs in time, students have to think about whether one event comes before or after another in time when placing them on the time line.

✓ *Group events by setting.*

Another strategy for accounting for shifts in time in passages is to record the events by time (for example, present day, age six, back to present day) or by place (for example, at home, at school, back at home). Using this strategy, students should realize that an event that happens the next day is not one that happens "right after" any other event:

FIGURE 7.5 **Time Line of Plot Events**

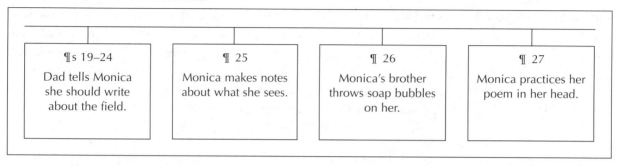

| ¶s 19–24 | ¶ 25 | ¶ 26 | ¶ 27 |
| Dad tells Monica she should write about the field. | Monica makes notes about what she sees. | Monica's brother throws soap bubbles on her. | Monica practices her poem in her head. |

What happens right after Dad tells Monica that she should write about the empty field?   (¶s 19–24)

  A Monica makes notes about what she sees.   (same day)

  B Monica practices her poem in her head.   (next day)

  C Monica's brother throws soap bubbles on her.   (same day)

  D Monica remembers her teacher's advice.   (same day)

Options A, C, and D happen the same day as the event in the stem and are therefore viable because one of them is likely to have happened "right after." Students can feel confident about ruling out option B because it happens much later in time.

Students can also track events by place:

What happens right after Dad tells Monica that she should write about the empty field?   (at field)

  A Monica makes notes about what she sees.   (at field)

  B Monica practices her poem in her head.   (at school)

  C Monica's brother throws soap bubbles on her.   (at home)

  D Monica remembers her teacher's advice.   (earlier)

Only option A happens in the same location as the event provided in the stem—and it makes sense, then, that one would happen right after the other. Students can feel confident about dismissing the other options based on this strategy.

It is important for students to have multiple, easy-to-use strategies when approaching chronology items, because some strategies will be more effective for eliminating viable options than others. That is, the paragraph reference and time line strategies help to eliminate option D. The strategy of recording events by time helps to eliminate option B. But the strategy of recording events by place is the most helpful because it eliminates options B, C, and D, leaving the one correct answer—option A.

Conclusion/Inference

Based on the poem that Monica's brother writes, the reader can tell that—

A he is not a good student in English class
B he is not serious about trying to help his sister
C he is sharing his favorite poem with his sister
D he is letting her use a poem that he wrote for school

Correct answer: B

Strategies

✓ *Recognize the item type.*

The phrase "the reader can tell" indicates that this item requires students—the readers—to draw a conclusion or make an inference; in other words, the answer is not stated in the passage.

Alternate versions of conclusion/inference items are presented in Figure 7.6.

✓ *Use information in the item stem as a clue to important information in the passage.*

Students who pay attention to the event referenced in the stem will be able to pinpoint the gen-

FIGURE 7.6 **Alternate Versions of Conclusion/Inference Items**

The reader can *tell* that _____ —

The reader can *conclude* that _____ —

The reader can *infer* that _____ —

It is *likely* that _____ —

The author *probably* thinks that _____ —

Based on information in the passage, it is *reasonable* to *conclude* that _____ —

The reader can *assume* that the author *probably* believes/thinks _____ because —

---

eral area in which the answer to the item can be surmised. The event is contained in the words *the poem that Monica's brother writes.*

Students should be able to track the text that relates to Monica's brother and the poem he offers her. (The "chunk, sum, and picture" strategy explained in Chapter 4 should help students find the information quickly.) Monica's brother appears in paragraphs 8–10 and 26. Monica's brother writes a poem that appears between paragraphs 9 and 10. Because these are the only places in which Monica's brother is referenced, students have the advantage of focusing solely on these sections of text to see what information they can uncover to determine the answer.

✓ *Build a case.*

Although conclusion/inference items will not be specifically stated in the passage, students should be able to mount evidence—in the form of events, details, characters' actions and reactions, and so forth—that indicates that one option is clearly right and the other three cannot be supported.

Students should be encouraged to try to build a case for each option. Doing so will help students develop an understanding that drawing conclusions/inferences is about stepping away from what the passage actually says and thinking about what those words actually mean. A key question for building a case for each option is, "What does the passage say about . . . ?", as shown in Figure 7.7.

By trying to build a case for each option, students should be able to determine that a great deal of information—a surprising amount, perhaps—can be attributed to the idea expressed in option B. Students can also find evidence to dismiss the other options.

FIGURE 7.7 **Building a Case**

What does the passage say about . . .	Evidence
A . . . Monica's brother not being a good student in English class?	Nothing. In fact, it doesn't make much sense that Monica would ask him for help if he is not a good student!
B . . . Monica's brother not being serious about helping his sister?	It says he snatches the notebook from her. It says he writes the poem quickly. It says he pitches the notebook back to her. The poem is a "roses are red" poem. The poem says, "I'm done with you!" in capital letters. It says he shoos Monica away. It says he goes back to listening to his music. It says Monica realizes that she should not have bothered him.
C . . . Monica's brother sharing his favorite poem with his sister?	Nothing. In fact, he writes the poem in front of her—so he is not sharing a poem he likes.
D . . . Monica's brother letting Monica use a poem that he wrote for school?	Nothing. In fact, this cannot be true! Monica's brother writes the poem in front of her—not in the past for a school assignment.

Prediction

Which of these will likely happen next?

A   Monica will receive an award from her teacher.

B   Monica will plant grass and flowers in the empty field.

C   Monica will enjoy sharing her poem with the class.

D   Monica will rewrite her poem.

Correct answer: C

Strategies

✓ *Recognize the item type.*

The words *will likely happen next* indicate that this item tests prediction.

Alternate versions of prediction items are presented in Figure 7.8.

✓ *Summarize how the passage ends.*

Because a prediction item usually asks about what will happen in the future, the natural starting place to ponder this item is at the end of the passage. It makes little sense to think about the beginning of the passage, because so much can happen and the main character can change in significant ways throughout the passage. In "Searching for an Idea," Monica changes from being frustrated to being pleased that she has managed to write a poem, so it makes sense that

FIGURE 7.8 **Alternate Versions of Prediction Items**

If the story had continued, what would *most likely have happened*?

In the future, Monica will likely _____.

What do you think will happen *the next time* [character's name] _____?

What *will probably happen* after _____?

readers would make predictions about Monica based on the latest information they know about her.

Students should focus their attention on the last couple of paragraphs to ponder what is likely to happen next. Rereading a significant chunk of the text's ending helps ground students; they will know what the main character is saying and doing when the story ends. So, before trying to determine a logical next step in the action, students should first summarize the last moments of the story. They might do so as follows:

> *Monica is excited to share her poem with the class. She is pleased that she has been able to find a subject and complete her poem.*

Once a summary is formulated, students can begin thinking through each answer choice.

✓ *Pick what is likely, not what is lovely!*

Prediction items tend to present events as options that are phrased in positive, "lovely" ways. For instance, option A, "Monica will receive an award from her teacher" certainly describes an event that students will find appealing; after all, what student wouldn't want his or her teacher's recognition and praise? And option B, "Monica will plant grass and flowers in the empty field," describes a lovely gesture.

The problem with these options is that there is little evidence to support that either will happen, given the direction of the plot. Perhaps these lovely events *could* happen, but students shouldn't argue themselves into believing that these events *will* happen. In a prediction item, the difference between discerning what *could* happen from what *will likely* happen is often the difference between getting the answer correct or incorrect.

Thus, students have to be on the lookout for events presented as options that readers *cannot know* as a result of what is told in the plot. While Monica seems to think her poem is great, readers cannot know whether the teacher has any intention of distributing one or more awards for good work. Because there is no mention of a contest or an award of any kind, option A is something readers cannot know.

Option B suggests that Monica is so displeased with the field being empty that she thinks she should plant grass and flowers there. But readers cannot know whether Monica has negative feelings about the emptiness of the field, because she does not express any such feelings; in fact, she probably views the field positively, because that field is the inspiration for her poem. Therefore, option B is something readers cannot know.

✓ *Build a case.*

For students who can weed out options using the strategies above but cannot decide between two options, building a case is always a good strategy. In this item, if students cannot decide between options C and D, they should return to the passage to find information to support each option, as shown in Figure 7.9.

Building a case helps students determine that there is information to support option C but not option D. In fact, students might also notice that the support for option C negates option D as viable, which is one benefit of trying to build a case for each option of an interpretation item. Option C is the clear correct answer.

FIGURE 7.9 **Building a Case**

Option	Evidence
C Monica will enjoy sharing her poem with the class.	Yes. Monica's hand shoots up when the teacher asks for volunteers, so readers know Monica is excited to share. Monica practices her poem in her head, so readers know Monica wants to read it well.
D Monica will rewrite her poem.	No. In fact, Monica is excited about her poem, so it doesn't make sense that she would want to change it.

Fact/Opinion

Which of these is an opinion in the passage?

A   *Monica told her dad about her big assignment.*

B   *"I have to write a poem for school," Monica said.*

C   *Monica looked out across the field again.*

D   *"You are good with words," her dad said.*

Correct answer: D

Strategies

✓ *Recognize the item type.*

The word *opinion* clearly indicates that this item tests students' ability to distinguish an opinion from facts.

✓ *Have anchor examples.*

When students see the word *fact* or *opinion* in an item stem, they should be taught explicitly that they are being asked to distinguish fact from opinion or opinion from fact. Therefore, in this item assessing the ability to identify an opinion, students should know that there will be only one opinion and that the other answer choices will contain facts.

To begin thinking about the distinction, students should recall a simple example of fact and opinion. For instance, a student might use anchor examples similar to these:

I was born on April 21, 1998. (fact)

Cleaning my room is a waste of time. (opinion)

From these examples, students can recognize that the first statement, a fact, can be verified, while the second statement is their opinion, but not likely the viewpoint of their parents! Students can then use what they glean about facts and opinions from the anchor examples to evaluate the options.

✓ *Look for signal words.*

Sometimes statements of opinion can be detected because of signal words and/or judgment words. Some signal words include *think, believe, suppose, feel, probably, perhaps, usually, sometimes,* and *often.* Some judgment words include *good, bad, great, best, worst,* and other such adjectives.

In this item, option A (*big*) and option D (*good*) use judgment words, so on appearance alone, these two options need further consideration.

✓ *Locate the statement in the passage to understand the context.*

In fact/opinion items, the four answer choices are statements from the passage that are plucked from their context. Many times, not having a good understanding of the context in which the statement is made adds to the difficulty of the item. Encourage students to find each option in the passage and mark the paragraph number:

A   *Monica told her dad about her big assignment.*   (¶ 4)

B   *"I have to write a poem for school," Monica said.*   (¶ 8)

C   *Monica looked out across the field again.*   (¶ 25)

D   *"You are good with words," her dad said.*   (¶ 6)

Then, simply reading the sentences that come before and after each answer choice can reacquaint students with the context and help reveal the statement as either a fact or an opinion.

✓ *Reread each paragraph but leave out the statement.*

Sometimes it is easier to figure out whether a statement is fact or opinion by thinking about what information would be missing if the author had left out the statement.

Students can reread the paragraph, skip over the statement that serves as the answer choice, and ask themselves, "Is a fact or opinion needed there?"

For instance, in option B, it is important for Monica to relate to her brother that she must write a poem for school; without this *fact*, her brother would not know why Monica is seeking his help.

In option D, it is important for Monica's dad to express his *opinion* about Monica's ability to do her assignment because it explains why he does not help her. Because he thinks she is good with words, his comment explains why he doesn't help her at that point.

✓ *Construct try-out sentences to detect the opinion statement.*

Simply adding a version of "It is someone's opinion that . . ." to each option can help students determine which statement best reflects an opinion:

A *It is Monica's opinion* that she tells her dad about her big assignment.
B *It is Monica's opinion* that she has to write a poem for school.
C *It is Monica's opinion* that she looks out across the field again.
D *It is Monica's dad's opinion* that Monica is good with words.

Trying out the options in this way helps students detect which statement is really an opinion and that the others are facts. Students should respond to the statement made in option A by saying, "No, it's not Monica's opinion. Monica actually does tell her dad about her assignment; that action is verifiable. A contains a fact." Students should respond to option B by saying, "No, it is not Monica's opinion. Monica actually does have to write a poem for school; that need is verifiable. B is a fact." For option C, Monica does really look across the field again, so that is a fact, not her opinion. Therefore, option D stands out as an opinion—Monica's dad believes Monica is good with words. That might not be Monica's opinion of herself, but it is her dad's opinion of her ability.

Supporting Evidence

Which sentence in the last paragraph best shows how Monica feels about the poem she has written?

A   *When her teacher asked for volunteers, Monica's hand shot up in a flash.*

B   *In her head, she practiced reading her poem to the class.*

C   *She thought about how her teacher was right.*

D   *A poem can be written about anything—even an empty field.*

Correct answer: A

Strategies

✓ *Recognize the item type.*

The words "Which sentence in the last paragraph best shows" and the italicized sentences in the options indicate to students that they must support an idea presented in the item stem with specific evidence from the passage. The words "shows how Monica feels" present the idea that must be supported by one of the four sentences that compose the options.

Alternate versions of supporting evidence items are presented in Figure 7.10.

✓ *Mark each option with its paragraph reference.*

For supporting evidence items, because the options are lifted from the passage, it is a good

idea to find them and mark the paragraph reference next to each option. Many times, not having a good understanding of the context for each sentence adds to the difficulty of the item. Students can find out whether the sentence connects with the idea in the item stem or not by reading the statements that come before and after each answer choice.

In this item, because all options come from paragraph 27, this strategy is not particularly helpful, because the options appear one after another in the same paragraph. Nonetheless, students can rely on the clues *within* the sentences themselves and in the paragraph overall. For instance, students should be able to use all the sentences in paragraph 27 to gain an understanding of how Monica feels at this point in the story.

✓ *Answer the question first and then look for a good match.*

Items that ask students to find supporting ideas for a particular conclusion or assertion have essentially two steps. The first step is to arrive at an answer to the question posed in the stem. In this case, What can readers conclude about how Monica's feeling about the poem she has written? The item stem does not provide this information or any clues about the answer; that is, there are no hints in the stem itself about Monica's feelings. So students can reread the paragraph (as suggested in the previous strategy) for hints. If students can decide on an answer and formulate it in their own words—for example, "Monica feels proud and excited"—then they can move on to finding a sentence that best reflects that feeling.

Taking that important first step means that students have a more critical eye to evaluate the options. Otherwise, the options might all look correct because they are connected in various ways to Monica's writing a poem: Monica *does*

FIGURE 7.10 **Alternate Versions of Supporting Evidence Items**

> Which detail about _____ is most important to the passage?
>
> Which information supports the conclusion that _____?

volunteer, Monica *does* think her teacher is right, Monica *does* learn that a poem can be written about anything. But the question posed in the stem is more pointed and asks for a specific feeling—and when students can make that determination before reading the options, they have more clarity about what they are hunting for. Therefore, this is an important first step that must not be overlooked. Then they can proceed to the second step, described in the next strategy.

✓ *Ask a key question.*

The second step is for students to use their response ("Monica feels proud and excited") to look for the sentence in the options that is the best match. Formulating their response as a key question can help:

A *When her teacher asked for volunteers, Monica's hand shot up in a flash.*
   Does this option show that Monica feels proud and excited? Yes.

B *In her head, she practiced reading her poem to the class.*
   Does this option show that Monica feels proud and excited? Yes. A little.

C *She thought about how her teacher was right.*
   Does this option show that Monica feels proud and excited? No.

D *A poem can be written about anything— even an empty field.*
   Does this option show that Monica feels proud and excited? No.

The key question should help students eliminate a few of the options, but it will not necessarily reveal one correct answer. Because the stem uses the word *best*, students have to assume that one answer is better than another and must come up with a reason to distinguish them. In this case, students will likely recognize that option A more specifically suggests Monica's pride and excitement because of her enthusiasm to share her poem with the class. Therefore, option A is the correct, the best, answer.

Chapter 8

Text Matters

This chapter presents information about the most common types of items used to assess text matters on state assessments. These include author's purpose, text type, and author's organization. The following are examples, not particular to any state, of reading standards for text matters. Students are expected to:

- identify an *author's purpose* for writing;
- identify the genre and *type of text* written by an author;
- recognize common patterns of *organization* (such as cause-effect, chronological, problem-solution) used by an author to express ideas.

Basic Strategies for Text Matters Items

The following basic strategies are good starting points for teachers to share with students as they work together to make sense of reading test items about text matters. Later in this chapter, strategies that are specific to certain types of text matters items are explored.

✓ *Recognize the item type.*

Author's purpose. Items assessing students' ability to identify an author's purpose for writing usually include the word *purpose* or the words *author's purpose* in the item stem. All options will be "purpose words." On elementary assessments, students are expected to know these purposes: define, describe, explain, inform, illustrate, demonstrate, compare, list, entertain, tell, persuade, and convince. Purpose items can ask about the entire passage, multiple paragraphs or a section of text, or a single paragraph of the passage.

Text type. Text type items are fairly straightforward, because the answer choices are composed of text types that are mentioned in the curriculum's reading standards and therefore should be familiar to students: realistic fiction, historical fiction, literary nonfiction (expository), biography, autobiography, drama, poetry, mystery, fantasy, myths, legends, fables, folktales, fairy tales, interviews, editorials, advertisements, and so forth.

More challenging text type items ask students to identify a possible appropriate book title or the type of source that the passage might appear in. For these items, students need to first decide the genre of the passage and then use information about the features of the genre and the content of the passage to determine the best choice.

Author's organization. Items assessing students' ability to recognize an organizational pattern usually include the words *organized* or *organization*. Organization items can cover the entire passage or can ask about a portion of the passage, the latter especially when authors change the pattern for a specific reason.

✓ *Have anchor examples.*

Author's purpose and text type. Students should learn to associate certain purposes with text types. For example, fact-based newspaper articles (text type) should be associated with the purpose *inform*; advertisements and editorials (text type) should be associated with the purpose *persuade*; instructional manuals should be associated with the purpose *explain* or *list steps*. Anchor examples that prepare students to recognize an author's purpose should be built around discussions about text types.

Author's organization. Some organizational patterns can be difficult to detect because they cannot be exclusively linked to certain text types (as is often the case with an author's purposes for writing). For instance, an informational passage might use a problem-solution or cause-effect structure, but a narrative passage could as well. Furthermore, students have to make sure to think about the *pattern* the author uses rather than the content of the ideas. For example, an author might talk about the cause of a problem within a text, but the structure might be chronological. As a result, students need many opportunities to analyze how an author organizes ideas within a text. Anchor examples for the most common organizational patterns can help students recognize these same structures in the passages they encounter on assessments.

✓ *Ask a key question.*

Posing a question using the defining features of the purpose, text type, and organization helps students put their thinking toward the correct answer. These three item types are actually related enough that students can use their knowledge about purpose to help with text type items and vice versa. Similarly, students' knowledge of text type can help them predict the author's purpose for writing and the patterns that the author might have used.

In order for students to be able to pose helpful questions, though, they need to have a good understanding of purpose words, text types, and organizational structures that may appear on an assessment. Test publishers usually take their leads from the ones that are specifically mentioned in the curriculum.

The activities presented in Section 4 about purpose, text type, and organization will also help arm students with the knowledge they will need to access these types of items.

Author's Purpose

What is the purpose of this passage?

A   To persuade
B   To inform
C   To entertain
D   To describe

Correct answer: C

Strategies

✓ *Recognize the item type.*

The word *purpose* indicates that this item tests an author's purpose for writing.

Alternate versions of purpose items are presented in Figure 8.1.

✓ *Have anchor examples.*

Some purposes are more difficult for students to understand than others, so discussions about an author's purpose are best tied to text types and features. In this case, students who have read widely in the genre of realistic fiction will likely

FIGURE 8.1 **Alternate Versions of Purpose Items**

NOTE: Answer choices are provided for one item to indicate what the options for purpose items generally look like.

The author probably wrote the passage to tell readers—

Why did the author most likely write the passage?

In paragraph X, the author _____ in order to—

Why does the author end the passage by _____?

Why does the author include paragraphs X and Y?

What is the purpose of the passage?

A   To persuade readers to try hard in school
B   To inform readers
C   To entertain readers
D   To describe how to write a poem

recognize the sample passage "Searching for an Idea" as a story with a scenario that could conceivably happen to someone. Anchor examples of various kinds of fiction should help students determine that the purpose of a story is usually to entertain.

Nonetheless, *to entertain* as an option can be difficult for students to apply, because they tend to think of entertainment as something that makes them laugh. But rarely are passages on reading assessments selected because they make students laugh! Some reshaping of the definition of *entertain* is needed in the minds of students in order for them to understand that *to entertain* as a purpose essentially means *to provide a pleasurable and/or easy read* and *to tell a story*. Students operating with these definitions should think of most stories on reading assessments—such as realistic fiction, fantasy, and so forth—as having the purpose *to entertain*.

The activity on pages 220–221 can help familiarize students with purpose words commonly used on an assessment.

✓ *Ask a key question.*

Students can think through the answer choices by posing a question about the key word in each option if they know simple definitions/features of those purposes:

A   Is this passage meant to persuade readers to do something?
B   Is this passage meant to tell readers how to do something or share facts about something important?
C   Is this passage meant to tell readers a story?
D   Is this passage meant to describe something important to readers?

By answering these questions, some purposes will be particularly easy to eliminate. For instance, option A, "to persuade" is a purpose that is often easy for students to detect because common persuasive texts such as advertisements, fliers, and editorials look and "sound" a certain way. The question "Is this passage meant to persuade readers to do something?" draws attention to the fact that the author does not tell Monica's story in an attempt to convince readers to take action on an issue.

Furthermore, this passage is a *story*, plain and simple. It is not remotely the kind of passage that provides facts (option B) or describes something (option D). Option C is the clear correct answer.

Text Type

The passage can best be described as—

A   mystery
B   tall tale
C   biography
D   realistic fiction

Correct answer: D

Strategies

✔ *Recognize the item type.*

While no clue words per se appear in the item stem, the fact that the item asks about what describes the passage as a whole, and that the four options comprise familiar text types, indicates that this item tests text type.

Alternate versions of text type items are presented in Figure 8.2.

✔ *Have anchor examples.*

Students should learn to associate certain features with text types. For instance, realistic fiction pieces should have a "that could happen" feel to them, while advertisements and editorials will contain persuasive language. Students who have read and discussed Kate DiCamillo's *Because of Winn-Dixie*, for instance, can use that text as an anchor example of realistic fiction. Students should be able to recognize that DiCamillo's novel has many of the same qualities as the passage "Searching for an Idea"—especially those that relate to important literary elements.

The activity on pages 221–222 can help provide students with anchor features and examples of various text types.

✔ *Ask a key question.*

Knowledge of basic definitions/features of the text types that are presented as answer choices can help students home in on the correct answer. Simple questions can be posed using the key word(s) in each option:

A   Are the events meant to be mysterious and are they impossible to explain?
B   Are the events exaggerated and impossible to achieve?
C   Do the events tell about the life of a real person?
D   Could the events happen to me or someone I know?

By answering these questions, most text types will be particularly easy to eliminate. For instance, option A, "mystery," seems especially wrong because there is nothing mysterious about any of the events in the passage, and the events are not exaggerated or impossible to achieve, as would be the case with option B, "tall tale." A quick way to eliminate option C, "biography," is to notice that Monica does not have a last name, and informational texts, such as biography, include the first and last name of the real person being written about.

Furthermore, students should recognize that this passage is a story, plain and simple, and be able to match that understanding to option D, "realistic fiction," as the clear correct answer.

FIGURE 8.2 **Alternate Versions of Text Type Items**

This passage could likely be found in a book titled—

This passage might be found in—

A   a collection of stories

B   a poetry book

C   a newspaper

D   an encyclopedia

Author's Organization

How is the passage mostly organized?

A Comparison and contrast
B Problem and solution
C Cause and effect
D Step-by-step instructions

Correct answer: B

Strategies

✓ *Recognize the item type.*

The word *organized* tells students that this item tests author's organization.

Alternate versions of author's organization items are presented in Figure 8.3.

✓ *Have anchor examples.*

Students need anchor examples that can help them determine the organization of a reading passage on an assessment. If, for instance, students choose Ken Mochizuki's *Baseball Saved Us* as an anchor example of the problem-solution organizational pattern, they should be able to make the connection that in this passage, a problem is introduced early on (Monica can't write a poem) and solved by the end (Monica is able to write her poem). Furthermore, students' anchor examples of the organizational patterns that compose the three distractors in this item should help students eliminate them as viable.

The activity on pages 223–224 can help to provide students with anchor features and examples.

✓ *Ask a key question.*

The answer choices for author's organization items contain key words that can be formulated into basic questions:

A Are two things being compared?
What two things are alike and different?

FIGURE 8.3 **Alternate Versions of Author's Organization Items**

The information in this passage is mainly organized—

A in order of importance
B in the order in which events happen
C by presenting a cause and then its effects
D by comparing two or more things

How is this passage organized?

A It tells a story.
B It gives a description of several places.
C It uses a question-and-answer format.
D It gives step-by-step instructions.

How are the first five paragraphs of the passage organized?

A A question is asked and then answered.
B Two sides of an issue are presented.
C Events are placed in the order they happened.
D Events are listed from most important to least important.

Which of the following best describes how the passage is organized?

A Sequential order
B Comparison and contrast
C Proposition and support
D Cause and effect

B Is there a problem?
What is the solution?
C Is there a stated or implied cause?
Are the effects explored or described?
D Are there instructions for something?
Is there a numbered list or bullets?

By posing questions, some organizational patterns will be particularly easy to eliminate. For instance, option D, "step-by-step instructions" is a structure that is easily recognizable because of specific features, such as numbers or time-order transitions (for example, the words *first* and *next*).

Because students will not be able to find evidence to answer the key questions posed for options A and C, they can determine that option B, "problem and solution," is the best answer.

✓ Find paragraph references using the "chunk" strategy.

Encourage students to find paragraph references for the patterns that are used as options in an author's organization item:

A Comparison and contrast   (nowhere)
B Problem and solution   (problem: ¶s 1–17
                             and solution: ¶s 18–27)
C Cause and effect   (nowhere)
D Step-by-step instructions   (nowhere)

Using the "chunk" strategy (explained in detail in Chapter 4), students can divide the passage into manageable chunks and more clearly see the organization of the passage. By determining that a problem is presented in paragraphs 1–17 and that the solution is explored in paragraphs 18–27, students will recognize option B as the clear correct answer.

Putting Strategies to Work

Strategies are meant to be used, otherwise they are of no use! This section is designed with that principle in mind—that students need high-quality test preparation materials to read, ponder, and explore as a genre so they can ultimately demonstrate their strategic thinking about reading and tests.

The materials in this section provide a variety of passages, short and long, that are similar to those that students will encounter on most state reading assessments. The passages include those in the genres of realistic fiction, biography, poetry, and practical/procedural/functional reading. (Paired passages are not featured, although they are included on the elementary levels of some reading assessments.) Following the passages are a variety of items from the categories explored in Section 2, which are the most commonly assessed standards on reading tests.

This section also contains teacher guides. Because teacher modeling of strategies for reading and test taking is valuable for students (Johnson 1998; Fuhrken and Roser, forthcoming), the guides are included to direct teachers as they work together with students to help them understand and apply the strategies explained in detail in Section 2. Each teacher guide is presented the same way: The sample item is listed and followed by a table in which the left column lists the strategies that students can use, and the right column describes the kind of thinking that students should do in order to apply each strategy. Teachers may decide to share all or just a few of the strategies for each item type. They might also use the materials to construct mini-lessons for each sample item or a particular strategy that is new to students. The goal of Section 3 is to provide an array of test preparation materials that teachers can tailor to their students' needs.

Additionally, this section ends with a reprint of the passage and sample items that are described in detail in Section 2. Teachers may want this material in a compact form so that they can use it as the basis of think-alouds, for mini-lessons, in literacy centers, or for other discussions with students as they build understandings of strategies that work.

"The Question" from *Frindle* by Andrew Clements

1   The first day of school was always a get-acquainted day. Books were passed out, and there was a lot of chatter. Everyone asked, "What did *you* do over the summer?"

2   Periods one through six went by very smoothly for Nick.

3   But then came period seven. Mrs. Granger's class was all business.

4   The first thing they did was take a vocabulary pretest to see how many of the thirty-five words for the week the kids already knew. *Tremble, circular, orchestra*—the list went on and on. Nick knew most of them.

5   Then there was a handout about class procedures. After that there was a review paper about cursive writing, and then there was a sample sheet showing how the heading should look on every assignment. No letup for thirty-seven minutes straight.

6   Nick was an expert at asking the delaying question—also known as the teacher-stopper, or the guaranteed-time-waster. At three minutes before the bell, in that split second between the end of today's class work and the announcement of tomorrow's homework, Nick could launch a question guaranteed to sidetrack the teacher long enough to delay or even wipe out the homework assignment.

7   Timing was important, but asking the right question—that was the hard part. Questions about stuff in the news, questions about the college the teacher went to, questions about the teacher's favorite book or sport or hobby—Nick knew all the tricks, and he had been very successful in the past.

8   Here he was in fifth grade, near the end of his very first language arts class with Mrs. Granger, and Nick could feel a homework assignment coming the way a farmer can feel a rainstorm.

9   Mrs. Granger paused to catch her breath, and Nick's hand shot up. She glanced down at her seating chart, and then up at him. Her sharp gray eyes were not even turned up to half power.

10   "Yes, Nicholas?"

11   "Mrs. Granger, you have so many dictionaries in this room, and that huge one especially . . . where did all those words come from? Did they just get copied from other dictionaries? It sure is a big book."

12   It was a perfect thought-grenade—KaPow!

13   Several kids smiled, and a few peeked at the clock. Nick was famous for this, and the whole class knew what he was doing.

14   Unfortunately, so did Mrs. Granger. She hesitated a moment, and gave Nick a smile that was just a little too sweet to be real. Her eyes were the color of a thundercloud.

15   "Why, what an interesting question, Nicholas. I could talk about that for hours, I bet." She glanced around the classroom. "Do the rest of you want to know, too?" Everyone nodded yes. "Very well then. Nicholas, will you do some research on that subject and give a little oral report to the class? If you find out the answer yourself, it will mean so much more than if I just told you. Please have your report ready for our next class."

16   Mrs. Granger smiled at him again. Very sweetly. Then it was back to business. "Now, the homework for tomorrow can be found on page twelve of your *Words Alive* book. . . ."

17   Nick barely heard the assignment. His heart was pounding, and he felt small, very small. He could feel the tops of his ears glowing red. A complete shutdown. An extra assignment. And probably a little black mark next to his name on the seating chart.

18   Everything he had heard about this teacher was true—don't mess around with The Lone Granger.

1. Which of these could be another title for this passage?

   A   "Nick's Plan Goes Wrong"
   B   "An Oral Report on Dictionaries"
   C   "Nick's Embarrassment"
   D   "A Teacher's Nickname"

2. How does Nick try to keep his class from receiving homework?

   A   He asks the teacher about her favorite book.
   B   He tells the teacher what he did over the summer.
   C   He asks the teacher about a big dictionary she has.
   D   He agrees to do an oral report the next day.

3. Paragraphs 3–5 present Mrs. Granger as—

   A   curious
   B   unfair
   C   playful
   D   demanding

4. The author uses the words "the first day of school" and "period seven" to indicate the—

   A   problem
   B   setting
   C   plot
   D   characters

5. Read this sentence from paragraph 15.

   "I could talk about that for hours, I bet."

   In this sentence, the author uses—

   A   alliteration
   B   hyperbole
   C   a simile
   D   rhyme

6. In paragraph 12, "a perfect thought-grenade" is a metaphor that shows—

   A   Nick is easily confused during language arts class
   B   Nick is trying to make his classmates laugh at him
   C   Nick thinks his comment has distracted the teacher
   D   Nick thinks he has done something to impress the teacher

7. Which of these is a result of trying to trick Mrs. Granger?

   A   Mrs. Granger gives Nick a special assignment.
   B   The class has to practice their cursive handwriting.
   C   Mrs. Granger goes over a handout about class procedures.
   D   The class has to do a homework assignment.

Teacher's Guide

"The Question" from *Frindle* by Andrew Clements

1. Which of these could be another title for this passage?

   A   "Nick's Plan Goes Wrong"
   B   "An Oral Report on Dictionaries"
   C   "Nick's Embarrassment"
   D   "A Teacher's Nickname"

Strategy	Explanation
✓ *Recognize the item type, locate important information in the item, and know the terms.*	This item tests understanding of summary. The words *another title* are clues to summarize the passage in a few words. A summary expresses the main ideas and most important details without including minor details.
✓ *Make the text more manageable with the "chunk, sum, and picture" strategy.*	The passage can be divided into these sections: What happens in seventh period; Nick asks a question; Nick's plan backfires; Nick realizes he shouldn't mess with Mrs. Granger.
✓ *Analyze each option for key words that relate to important literary elements.*	A "Nick's [character] Plan [plot] Goes Wrong" [problem] (¶s 6–18) B "An Oral Report on Dictionaries" [problem] (¶ 15) C "Nick's [character] Embarrassment" [detail] (¶ 17) D "A Teacher's Nickname" [detail] (¶ 18)

Correct answer: A. "Nick's Plan Goes Wrong" captures many literary elements and summarizes the story more fully than the other options.

2. How does Nick try to keep his class from receiving homework?

   A He asks the teacher about her favorite book.
   B He tells the teacher what he did over the summer.
   C He asks the teacher about a big dictionary she has.
   D He agrees to do an oral report the next day.

Strategy	Explanation
✓ *Recognize the item type and know the literary elements.*	This item tests understanding of plot. Although the word *plot* is not used, the event specified in the stem is a clue that this is a plot item. Plot items assess the relationships among major events in the passage.
✓ *Find the events in the passage and look for connection and truth.*	All options will come from ideas in the passage, but the wrong ones will not be related to or will misrepresent the event in the stem.
	How does Nick try to keep his class from receiving homework? (¶s 8–13) A He asks the teacher about her favorite book. (¶ 7—but this is what Nick has done *in the past.*) B He tells the teacher about what he did over the summer. (¶ 1—but this is what the *kids* do, not what Nick tells his teacher.) C He asks the teacher about a big dictionary she has. (¶ 11) D He volunteers to do an oral report the next day. (¶ 15—but Nick doesn't volunteer; his teacher makes him agree to do an oral report.)

Correct answer: C. Only option C is a plot event that is connected to the event posed in the stem and is represented accurately.

3. Paragraphs 3–5 present Mrs. Granger as—

    A curious
    B unfair
    C playful
    D demanding

Strategy	Explanation
✓ *Recognize the item type.*	This item tests understanding of character. "Mrs. Granger" in the stem and the "feeling words" of the options are clues that this is a character item.
✓ *Ask a key question.*	A What does Mrs. Granger do that presents her as curious? (Nothing.) B What does Mrs. Granger do that presents her as unfair? (Nothing.) C What does Mrs. Granger do that presents her as playful? (Nothing.) D What does Mrs. Granger do that presents her as demanding? (*all business; pretest; class procedures; cursive writing; heading; no letup*)

Correct answer: D. The descriptions in paragraphs 3–5 portray Mrs. Granger as demanding.

4. The author uses the words "the first day of school" and "period seven" to indicate the—

   A   problem
   B   setting
   C   plot
   D   characters

Strategy	Explanation
✓ *Recognize the item type.*	This item tests understanding of setting. The options are clues that this is an identification item.
✓ *Ask a key question.*	Students can use basic definitions of story elements to form questions: A Do the words indicate a conflict between characters? (No.) B Do the words tell when and where something happens? (Yes. It is the first day of school [when], and Nick is in seventh period class [where].) C Do the words tell about events? (No.) D Do the words tell about more than one character? (No.)

Correct answer: B. Knowledge of literary elements allows students to determine that the author is establishing when and where the story takes place, which is the setting.

5. Read this sentence from paragraph 15.

   "I could talk about that for hours, I bet."

   In this sentence, the author uses—

   A   alliteration
   B   hyperbole
   C   a simile
   D   rhyme

Strategy	Explanation
✓ *Recognize the item type and know common literary techniques well.*	This item tests understanding of hyperbole. The options are clues that this is an identification item. Students need to know literary techniques well and recall that hyperbole is exaggeration.
✓ *Have anchor examples.*	Anchor examples can help students think about the features of the literary techniques that are presented as options in this item.
✓ *Ask a key question (or four).*	Basic definitions of literary techniques can help students think about each option: A Do two or more words have the same beginning sound? (No.) B Is there exaggeration? (Yes. No one really desires to talk about one topic for hours.) C Is there a comparison using *like* or *as*? (No.) D Do two or more words rhyme? (No.)

Correct answer: B. Recalling basic definitions of literary techniques along with anchor examples should help students identify the targeted sentence as hyperbole.

6. In paragraph 12, "a perfect thought-grenade" is a metaphor that shows—

A   Nick is easily confused during language arts class
B   Nick is trying to make his classmates laugh at him
C   Nick thinks his comment has distracted the teacher
D   Nick thinks he has done something to impress the teacher

Strategy	Explanation
✓ *Recognize the item type, locate important information in the item, and know common literary techniques well.*	This item tests understanding of metaphor. The stem identifies a metaphor and asks students for an interpretation. Students need to recall that a metaphor is a direct comparison.
✓ *Use context clues.*	The metaphor can be found in paragraph 12, as stated in the stem. Rereading establishes the context, which is that Nick is asking a question to interrupt Mrs. Granger before she gives a homework assignment.
✓ *Ask key questions.* *1. What is being compared? 2. What is the writer saying these two things have in common?*	*Nick's question* is being compared to a *grenade*. Because a grenade blows things up, Nick's question "blows up" the teacher's "thought"—meaning that what the teacher is saying or is about to say is destroyed. The image is negative, so options A and C seem the most viable because they are stated negatively.
✓ *Build a case for each option.*	A Nick is easily confused during language arts class. (No evidence. Nick is not confused; he knows exactly what he is doing.) B Nick is trying to make his classmates laugh at him. (No evidence. Nick is not trying to amuse the class; he is trying to keep them from getting homework.) C Nick thinks his comment has distracted the teacher. (Supported. Beginning with paragraph 6, the author explains the goal of Nick's question is to distract the teacher—so that she won't give homework.) D Nick thinks he has done something to impress the teacher. (No evidence. Nick is not trying to impress the teacher.)

Correct answer: C. The context shows that the "thought-grenade" is the effect that Nick's question is intended to have on the teacher. By evaluating the comparison in the metaphor, noticing the negative meaning, and hunting for evidence, students should select option C as the clear correct answer.

7. Which of these is a result of trying to trick Mrs. Granger?

A   Mrs. Granger gives Nick a special assignment.
B   The class has to practice their cursive handwriting.
C   Mrs. Granger goes over a handout about class procedures.
D   The class has to do a homework assignment.

Strategy	Explanation
✓ *Recognize the item type.*	This items tests understanding of cause-effect. The word *result* in the item stem indicates that this is a cause-effect item.
✓ *Figure out which part of the relationship is provided.*	The cause is provided in the stem—Nick tries to trick Mrs. Granger. The effect is the answer.
✓ *Locate the events in the stem and the options in the passage.*	Trying to trick Mrs. Granger (¶ 11) A Mrs. Granger gives Nick a special assignment. (¶ 15) B The class has to practice their cursive handwriting. (¶ 5) C Mrs. Granger goes over a handout about class procedures. (¶ 5) D The class has to do a homework assignment. (¶ 16) Because cause-effect relationships usually appear close together, the paragraph references help students surmise that options A and D are the most viable.
✓ *Ask a key question.*	Ask, "Does trying to trick Mrs. Granger **cause** . . . A . . . Mrs. Granger to give Nick a special assignment? (Yes. His assignment is a direct result of the question he asks when he tries to distract her.) B . . . the class to practice their cursive handwriting? (No. This happens earlier.) C . . . Mrs. Granger to go over the class procedures? (No. This happens earlier.) D . . . the class to look up vocabulary words? (No. Mrs. Granger has planned the homework anyway. Trying to trick her just delays receiving the assignment.)

Correct answer: A. Recognizing the parts of the cause-effect relationship, locating the events in the passage, and questioning the relationship formed with each option reveal that option A is the clear correct answer.

"The Rail-Splitter" from *A Three-Minute Speech: Lincoln's Remarks at Gettysburg* by Jennifer Armstrong

1   When Abraham Lincoln was a boy in the Kentucky wilderness, he didn't have much time for school. Life on a farm meant hard work and plenty of it for a strong boy. Lincoln grew to manhood without spending much time at a schoolroom desk. He had an education in splitting fence rails and plowing fields, but not much book learning. That is not to say that he wasn't a smart man—he just wasn't an educated man, and there's a big difference.

2   The family moved from Kentucky to Indiana, and finally to Illinois when Lincoln was a young man. His first taste of leadership came when he volunteered in the Illinois militia and was elected captain of his company. After that he decided he'd like to try his hand at politics. In 1832 he ran for a seat in the Illinois House of Representatives. He failed. Two years later he ran again, and won. That was the first of four terms in a row.

3   It was while he was serving in the Illinois legislature that Lincoln decided he'd like to study to become a lawyer. He had a lawyer's logical mind, and he had a special knack for proving his side of an argument. Step by step by step, he could lay out the facts in a clear and uncomplicated way until soon enough he'd have everyone convinced. He was a natural persuader and a gifted storyteller. Years of farming had given him an appreciation for plain talk, and he would far rather earn his bread by arguing and debating than by splitting fence rails or plowing fields.

4   In some ways Lincoln was an unlikely person to succeed as a public speaker. He was tall and awkward and held himself in a hunched posture. He had a high, raspy voice and a backwoods Kentucky accent that made him sound like a country bumpkin. He tended to wave his hands around in the air as he spoke. He was not a good-looking man. Many people, when they saw him for the first time, had pretty low expectations.

5   But without fail his audiences perked up as they listened to what he actually *said* in that high and raspy voice. He was so sensible. So logical. So plainspoken. So funny. And so *smart*. If Abraham Lincoln had set out to prove that the sun shone at night and the moon was made of buttermilk biscuits, he probably could have talked people into believing it.

1. In which word does –er mean the same as it does in the word storyteller?

   A Quicker
   B Perhaps
   C Worker
   D Erase

2. Read the dictionary entry below.

   company [kuhm'-puh-nee] *n.* 1. a group of guests brought together for a social purpose 2. a number of people united to operate a business 3. a unit of soldiers or troops 4. companionship provided by a close friend

   Which definition best matches how the word company is used in paragraph 2?

   A Definition 1
   B Definition 2
   C Definition 3
   D Definition 4

3. What is the main idea of the first paragraph?

   A Despite having to work instead of going to school, Lincoln was smart.
   B Because Lincoln was strong as a boy, he was able to do a man's job.
   C Lincoln spent his early years in life in Kentucky.
   D Lincoln was good at splitting fence rails and plowing fields.

4. In the phrase "first taste of leadership" in paragraph 2, the word taste refers to—

   A an experience
   B disappointment
   C confusion
   D a message

5. Use this diagram to answer the following question.

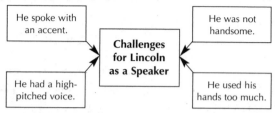

   Which of these can best be added to the web?

   A He did not often attend school.
   B He was awkward physically.
   C He failed in his first try at politics.
   D He talked plainly.

6. Which sentence from the passage is used to emphasize that Lincoln was persuasive?

   A *That is not to say that he wasn't a smart man—he just wasn't an educated man, and there's a big difference.*
   B *His first taste of leadership came when he volunteered in the Illinois militia and was elected captain of his company.*
   C *In some ways Lincoln was an unlikely person to succeed as a public speaker.*
   D *If Abraham Lincoln had set out to prove that the sun shone at night and the moon was made of buttermilk biscuits, he probably could have talked people into believing it.*

7. The information in the passage is organized—

   A by presenting a problem and then the solution
   B by stating a cause and then its effects
   C from most important to least important
   D in the order in which the events take place

8. Which of these best describes this passage?

   A Biography
   B Realistic fiction
   C Tall tale
   D Historical fiction

Teacher's Guide

"The Rail-Splitter" from *A Three-Minute Speech: Lincoln's Remarks at Gettysburg* by Jennifer Armstrong

1. In which word does –<u>er</u> mean the same as it does in the word <u>storyteller</u>?

    A Quicker
    B Perhaps
    C Worker
    D Erase

Strategy	Explanation
✓ *Locate important information in the item.*	This item tests understanding of suffixes. The stem indicates, with the underlining of a word part, that the suffix *-er* is being tested.
✓ *Look for familiar word parts and know common suffixes well.*	By drawing a vertical line to separate the letters *er* in each option (for example, quick | er), students can focus their attention on these letters and determine that only options A and C feature suffixes.
✓ *Have an anchor example.*	An anchor word such as *farmer* will help students figure out that *-er* means *someone who does a job*. Students could also look for other words with *-er* in the passage; in paragraph 4, *speaker* tells students that a speaker is *someone who speaks* (as a job). So, *worker* and *storyteller* are both nouns describing *someone who does*. In *quicker*, the suffix means *having more*, which is not the meaning that *–er* adds to *storyteller*.

Correct answer: C. Recognizing the item as testing understanding of suffixes, splitting apart the options to look for the correct use of the suffix, and using an anchor example or a structurally similar word in the passage help students determine that option C is correct.

2. Read the dictionary entry below.

company [kuhm'-puh-nee] *n.* 1. a group of guests brought together for a social purpose 2. a number of people united to operate a business 3. a unit of soldiers or troops 4. companionship provided by a close friend

Which definition best matches how the word <u>company</u> is used in paragraph 2?

A   Definition 1
B   Definition 2
C   Definition 3
D   Definition 4

Strategy	Explanation
✓ *Recognize the item type and locate important information in the item.*	This item tests understanding of a multiple-meaning word. The dictionary entry indicates that this item features a multiple-meaning word, which appears in paragraph 2. Because all entries are for the noun form, students cannot use their knowledge of parts of speech to eliminate any options.
✓ *Don't be enticed by the most familiar definition.*	Students likely know definition 1; they should not be drawn to it just because it is familiar to them.
✓ *Reread the targeted paragraph and use context clues to find a synonym.*	Rereading paragraph 2 helps to identify two clues: the word *militia* (which is like *military*) and the word *captain*. A good synonym might be *troop*.
✓ *Construct try-out sentences with a key word from each dictionary entry.*	Inserting a key word from each entry into the tested sentence looks like this: A . . . was elected captain of his <u>guests</u> B . . . was elected captain of his <u>business</u> C . . . was elected captain of his <u>soldiers</u> D . . . was elected captain of his <u>friend</u> Option C makes sense, given the context.

Correct answer: C. Recognizing the task based on the item type, finding context clues, selecting a synonym, and using a key word to try out each dictionary entry reveal that option C is the best answer.

3. What is the main idea of the first paragraph?

   A Despite having to work instead of going to school, Lincoln was smart.
   B Because Lincoln was strong as a boy, he was able to do a man's job.
   C Lincoln spent his early years in life in Kentucky.
   D Lincoln was good at splitting fence rails and plowing fields.

Strategy	Explanation
✓ *Recognize the item type and locate important information in the item.*	This item tests understanding of main idea. The stem indicates the type of item (key words: *main idea*) and the tested paragraph (paragraph 1).
✓ *Think big, not small.*	Option C does not sound "weighty." While paragraph 1 is about Lincoln's early life, option C is too general. Option D is a minor detail—it supports the more important idea that Lincoln worked hard as a boy.
✓ *Ask a critical question.*	By asking, "What is the one thing the author needs me to know?", students should recognize that the most important part of paragraph 1 is that Lincoln didn't have the opportunity to attend school often.
✓ *Look for evidence supporting the key words in the options.*	Students can isolate the key words in each option and search for supporting information: A having to work / instead of going to school / smart (sentences 1, 2, 3, 4, 5—every sentence!) B strong as a boy / able to do a man's job (sentence 2) C early years in life in Kentucky (sentence 1) D splitting rails / plowing fields (sentence 4)

Correct answer: A. The key words *main idea* tell what kind of item it is. A couple of the options can be eliminated because they are small ideas and are minor details. By looking for evidence of the key words in each option, students should select option A as the correct answer.

4. In the phrase "first taste of leadership" in paragraph 2, the word <u>taste</u> refers to—

    A an experience
    B disappointment
    C confusion
    D a message

Strategy	Explanation
✓ *Locate important information in the item and recognize the item type.*	This item tests understanding of figurative language. Students have to make the connection that the use of the word *taste* in the tested phrase is not literal; looking at the options helps.
✓ *Get a general feeling for the use of figurative language and use context clues.*	*Taste* can have either a positive or negative meaning, so readers have to reread paragraph 2 to realize Lincoln is portrayed in a positive light. Options B and C, which are negative feelings, are not likely viable.
✓ *Use substitution.*	Substitution works well because the tested word and the options are the same part of speech. Option A, "experience," makes sense, given the clues "volunteered" and "elected captain of his company"; the militia was his first *experience* with leadership.

Correct answer: A. While a variety of strategies can be used with figurative language items, context clues and substitution should easily lead students to the correct answer, option A.

5. Use this diagram to answer the following question.

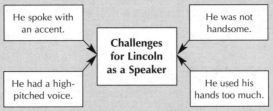

Which of these can best be added to the web?

A   He did not often attend school.
B   He was awkward physically.
C   He failed in his first try at politics.
D   He talked plainly.

Strategy	Explanation
✓ *Be familiar with a variety of graphic organizers and how they are read.*	This item tests understanding of how to interpret graphic organizers. This web has a central idea ("Challenges for Lincoln as a Speaker"), and the task is to add a supporting idea.
✓ *Use the "chunk, sum, and picture" strategy.*	The "chunk, sum, and picture" strategy should lead students to paragraph 4, which is about Lincoln as a speaker. The web's details are also from paragraph 4.
✓ *Eliminate options that are not absolutely true and think about how each option connects to the main topic.*	A He did not often attend school. (Not connected. This idea is presented earlier.) B He was awkward physically. (Supported in paragraph 4 with the words "awkward" and "had a hunched posture.") C He failed in his first try at politics. (Not connected. The passage says Lincoln failed at his first try at politics before his challenges are described.) D He talked plainly. (Talking plainly is a good thing, not a challenge.)

Correct answer: B. With experience reading graphic organizers, knowledge of the text content and structure/chronology (through the "chunk, sum, and picture" strategy), and a focus on the ideas in paragraph 4, students should easily recognize the correct answer, option B.

6. Which sentence from the passage is used to emphasize that Lincoln was persuasive?

    A   *That is not to say that he wasn't a smart man—he just wasn't an educated man, and there's a big difference.*

    B   *His first taste of leadership came when he volunteered in the Illinois militia and was elected captain of his company.*

    C   *In some ways Lincoln was an unlikely person to succeed as a public speaker.*

    D   *If Abraham Lincoln had set out to prove that the sun shone at night and the moon was made of buttermilk biscuits, he probably could have talked people into believing it.*

Strategy	Explanation
✓ *Locate important information in the item and recognize the item type.*	This item tests understanding of supporting evidence. The words *from the passage* and the italicized print indicate that the sentences used as options appear in the passage. Students must select the sentence that best supports the central idea of the stem (that Lincoln was persuasive).
✓ *Mark each option with its paragraph reference.*	A (¶ 1) B (¶ 2) C (¶ 4) D (¶ 5) After finding the sentences, students can use the context to identify synonyms or other ideas that depict Lincoln as persuasive. Because paragraph 5 is mostly about Lincoln's influence on people, the sentence from that paragraph is likely the answer (option D).
✓ *Ask a key question.*	After reading each option, students can ask, "Does this sentence show that Lincoln was persuasive?" A (No relationship.) B (No relationship. Lincoln would not need to be persuasive to be a volunteer.) C (No relationship. The words "unlikely person to succeed" definitely do not suggest that Lincoln was persuasive.) D (Yes. The words "could have talked people into believing" suggest persuasiveness.)

Correct answer: D. Finding the quoted sentences in the passage and using text clues and critical thinking should help students reason that option D is the best supporting sentence.

7. The information in the passage is organized—

A by presenting a problem and then the solution
B by stating a cause and then its effects
C from most important to least important
D in the order in which the events take place

Strategy	Explanation
✓ *Recognize the item type.*	This item tests understanding of author's organization. The key word in the stem is *organized*.
✓ *Have anchor examples and ask a key question.*	Students can use their anchor examples and knowledge of features to ask a key question: A Does the author present a problem about Lincoln and offer a solution? B Is there a cause and effect presented about Lincoln? C Is the information about Lincoln at the beginning most important and the information at the end least important? D Is the information about Lincoln presented in the order that it happened in his life?
✓ *Find paragraph references using the "chunk" strategy.*	Using the "chunk" strategy, students will not likely find a problem or a cause identified; therefore, options A and B are not viable. The three main chunks might be early life, beginning of career, and success later in career—suggesting a chronological sequence.

Correct answer: D. Students should be able to draw on their wide reading to recognize this pattern of organization as chronological. Key questions and the "chunk" strategy should also direct students to option D as the correct answer.

8. Which of these best describes this passage?

A   Biography
B   Realistic fiction
C   Tall tale
D   Historical fiction

Strategy	Explanation
✓ *Recognize the item type.*	This item tests understanding of text type. While the item stem does not contain specific clues, the options reveal that the item assesses knowledge of text type.
✓ *Have anchor examples.*	Recalling anchor examples and considering the features of those text types will help students eliminate several or all of the wrong options.
✓ *Ask a key question.*	A Do the events tell about the life of a real person? (Yes.) B Do the believable events happen to a character, not a real person? (No.) C Are the events exaggerated and impossible to achieve? (No.) D Are the events from the past both factual and fictional? (No.)

Correct answer: A. Recognizing the item type, having familiarity with all the text types, using anchor examples, and asking key questions about the features of the text types should help students determine that option A is the only possible answer.

"Squished Squirrel Poem" from *A Writing Kind of Day: Poems for Young Poets* by Ralph Fletcher

I wanted to write about
a squished squirrel
I saw on the road
near my house last week.

5   You can't write a poem
about a squished squirrel,
my teacher said to me.
I mean, you just can't do it.

Pick a sunrise or an eagle
10   or a dolphin, he suggested.
Pick something noble
to lift the human spirit.

I tried. I really did. But I kept
coming back to that squirrel.
15   Did his wife send him out
to fetch some food or something?

There was blood and guts
but here's what really got me:
he had pretty dark eyes
20   and they glistened still.

You can't write a poem
about a squished squirrel,
my teacher insisted,
but I don't think that's true.

1. In line 23, what does the word <u>insisted</u> mean?

   A   Wondered
   B   Commanded
   C   Hoped
   D   Accepted

2. What is the speaker's main problem?

   A   The speaker wants a squirrel as a pet.
   B   The speaker does not want to write a poem.
   C   The teacher does not believe the speaker's story about the squirrel.
   D   The teacher wants the speaker to write about something other than a squirrel.

3. Which line contains an example of alliteration?

   A   Line 6
   B   Line 9
   C   Line 17
   D   Line 18

4. What theme is suggested in the last stanza?

   A   People are willing to help when you need them the most.
   B   Getting used to something new takes time.
   C   Stay firm in your belief if it is important to you.
   D   Facing challenges can teach you about yourself.

5. What can the reader infer about the speaker?

   A   The speaker feels responsible for what has happened to the squirrel.
   B   The speaker has written several poems about a squirrel for the teacher in the past.
   C   The speaker wants the teacher's help to write a poem about a squirrel.
   D   The speaker has thought a great deal about the squirrel since seeing it.

Teacher's Guide

"Squished Squirrel" from *A Writing Kind of Day: Poems for Young Poets* by Ralph Fletcher

1. In line 23, what does the word <u>insisted</u> mean?

   A   Wondered
   B   Commanded
   C   Hoped
   D   Accepted

Strategy	Explanation
✓ *Locate important information in the item.*	This item tests understanding of how to use context clues. In the item stem, the underlining of *insisted* and the word *mean* identify this item as testing vocabulary/context clues.
✓ *Reread the targeted stanza and know a variety of context clues.*	The word *insisted* follows something the teacher says, so the tested word must be a way of speaking. Other descriptive clues indicate that the teacher has a definite opinion: "You can't write a poem about a squished squirrel" (stanza 2). Stanza 6 is the second time that the teacher says this, so *insisted* must mean *commanded*.
✓ *Use substitution to confirm the answer.*	Substitution works easily because the tested word and the options are the same part of speech. Given the context, *commanded* makes the most sense. *Wondered, hoped*, and *accepted* seem contrary to what the teacher thinks.

Correct answer: B. Through descriptive clues and the substitution strategy, students should determine that *insisted* means *commanded*, making B the correct answer.

2. What is the speaker's main problem?

A   The speaker wants a squirrel as a pet.
B   The speaker does not want to write a poem.
C   The teacher does not believe the speaker's story about the squirrel.
D   The teacher wants the speaker to write about something other than a squirrel.

Strategy	Explanation
✓ *Recognize the item type.*	This item tests understanding of conflict. The key word in the stem is *problem*.
✓ *Weed out problems that aren't problems.*	Students should try to weed out weak or unsupported options. Option A is obviously wrong because wanting a pet is not mentioned. Options B, C, and D at least "sound" like possible conflicts. But option B seems opposite of the speaker's problem because he does want to write a poem. Option C is not what the teacher complains about, nor can this idea be inferred.
✓ *Use the structure and title as clues.*	The problem is usually presented early in a text. The poem begins, "I wanted to write about a squished squirrel." The second stanza says, "You can't . . ." Putting together these ideas reveals the conflict. (And stanza 3 describes what the teacher wants the speaker to do instead.)

Correct answer: D. Because the problem is stated from the outset, students will likely recognize the clues that point to option D as the answer.

3. Which line contains an example of alliteration?

   A   Line 6
   B   Line 9
   C   Line 17
   D   Line 18

Strategy	Explanation
✓ *Recognize the item type and know common literary techniques well.*	This item tests understanding of alliteration. The key word in the stem is *alliteration*. Students need to recall the definition of alliteration—the repetition of the initial sound in two or more words.
✓ *Have an anchor example.*	An anchor example such as the book title *Some Smug Slug* can help students remember what alliteration is.
✓ *Underline, underline, underline.*	Underlining the first letter of the words in each option should easily reveal the answer: A <u>a</u>bout <u>a</u> <u>s</u>quished <u>s</u>quirrel B <u>P</u>ick <u>a</u> <u>s</u>unrise <u>or</u> <u>an</u> <u>e</u>agle C <u>T</u>here <u>was</u> <u>b</u>lood <u>an</u>d guts D but <u>h</u>ere's <u>w</u>hat <u>r</u>eally got <u>m</u>e

Correct answer: A. Familiarity with the technique and having an anchor example should lead students to use the underline strategy, which shows that option A is the answer.

4. What theme is suggested in the last stanza?

    A   People are willing to help when you need them the most.
    B   Getting used to something new takes time.
    C   Stay firm in your belief if it is important to you.
    D   Facing challenges can teach you about yourself.

Strategy	Explanation
✓ *Recognize the item type.*	This item tests understanding of theme. The item type, theme, is clearly identified in the stem.
✓ *Focus on key words.*	Key words can be found in each option: A help B getting used to something new C believing in something important to you D challenges teach you about yourself
✓ *Ask key questions.*	Students can consider if the options relate to the speaker: A Does the speaker receive <u>help</u>? B Does the speaker have to <u>get used to something new</u>? C Should the speaker <u>believe in something that is important to him</u>? D Does the speaker <u>overcome a challenge</u> and <u>learn something</u>?
✓ *Build a case.*	In the last stanza, the words "but I don't think that's true" suggest the speaker wants to pursue what is important to him, which is writing about a squirrel that affected him deeply.

Correct answer: C. Isolating key words, asking key questions, and building a case for each option help students determine that option C states a theme that can be supported.

5. What can the reader infer about the speaker?

   A The speaker feels responsible for what has happened to the squirrel.
   B The speaker has written several poems about a squirrel for the teacher in the past.
   C The speaker wants the teacher's help to write a poem about a squirrel.
   D The speaker has thought a great deal about the squirrel since seeing it.

Strategy	Explanation
✓ *Recognize the item type.*	This word tests understanding of inference. The word *infer* in the stem indicates this item requires inferring (rather than locating stated) information.
✓ *Use information in the item as a clue to important information in the passage.*	Students can ask themselves about the central idea in each option as it relates to the speaker: A Does the speaker express personal responsibly? B What does the speaker say that indicates that he has written about a squirrel previously? C Which part of the poem expresses the speaker's need for help from the teacher? D Is there evidence that the speaker has thought about the squirrel since seeing it?
✓ *Build a case.*	A (No evidence. The words "last week" in stanza 1 tell when this happened, so the speaker isn't responsible.) B (No evidence.) C (No evidence. It doesn't make sense that the speaker would want help from the person who says he can't write about a squirrel.) D (Supported. The speaker says, "I kept coming back to that squirrel." The speaker wonders, "Did his wife send him out to fetch some food or something?" The speaker describes the squirrel in stanza 5. These pieces of evidence all indicate the speaker has thought about the squirrel.)

Correct answer: D. Knowing that the answer must be inferred, the students can focus on the central idea and try to build a case for each option. Only the inference in option D can be supported sufficiently with evidence from the poem.

Making a Lollipop Bouquet:
A Craft Project for a Rainy Saturday

Here's What You'll Need:

Small flower pot (any color)
Green foam block
Pencil
Scissors
Green marker
About 20 lollipops (all the same size but different colors)

Here's What You Should Do:

1. Gather all the supplies. A green foam block is a special material that can be purchased at an art supply store or your local flower shop.

2. Place the green foam block on a flat surface. Turn the flower pot upside down and place it on top of the green foam block.

3. Use the pencil to outline the top of the flower pot on the green foam block. Stand the flower pot upright again.

4. Use scissors to cut the green foam block along the outline.

5. Gently place the green foam into the top of the flower pot. Adjust the foam slightly until it is level with the top of the flower pot.

6. Color a lollipop stick with the marker to make it appear green like a flower stem. Take the lollipop and place it at the center of the foam. Push the lollipop into the foam until only half of the lollipop stick shows.

7. Continue coloring the lollipop sticks and pushing the lollipops into the foam, leaving very little room between the lollipops. Adjust the design as needed so that the lollipops resemble flowers growing in the pot.

8. Decide whose day will be brightened by receiving your lollipop bouquet and present it to this person.

1. What step comes immediately after putting the flower pot on top of the green foam block?

   A   Cutting the green foam block

   B   Pushing the lollipops into the green foam

   C   Drawing the shape of the flower pot on the green foam

   D   Placing the green foam gently into the top of the flower pot

2. The author likely thinks that the reader might not have experience with which of the supplies?

   A   A flower pot

   B   A green foam block

   C   A pencil

   D   A green marker

3. The reader can infer that the green foam is important in the craft project because it—

   A   prevents the flower pot from tipping over

   B   keeps the lollipops in their proper place

   C   is meant to look like grass growing in the pot

   D   is the same color as the lollipop sticks

4. What is the purpose of the passage?

   A   To entertain

   B   To persuade

   C   To compare

   D   To explain

5. What is the purpose of the numbered section of the craft project?

   A   It tells how to put together the bouquet.

   B   It lists the supplies needed to make the bouquet.

   C   It makes suggestions about where to find a bouquet.

   D   It tells what to do with the bouquet.

Teacher's Guide

"Making a Lollipop Bouquet: A Craft Project for a Rainy Saturday"

1. What step comes immediately after putting the flower pot on top of the green foam block?

   A   Cutting the green foam block
   B   Pushing the lollipops into the green foam
   C   Drawing the shape of the flower pot on the green foam
   D   Placing the green foam gently into the top of the flower pot

Strategy	Explanation
✓ *Recognize the item type.*	This item tests understanding of chronology. The words *immediately after* indicate chronology.
✓ *Locate the event in the stem and the options in the passage.*	Stem: putting pot on foam block (step 2) A cutting foam block (step 4) B pushing in lollipops (step 6) C drawing shape on pot (step 3) D placing foam into pot (step 5)
✓ *Use the chronology (steps) to find the answer.*	Because steps are chronological and the event in the stem is in step 2, the answer must be the event in step 3.

Correct answer: C. Noticing that the item is testing understanding of chronology and finding the event in the stem and in all options are the keys to determining the correct answer, which is option C.

2. The author likely thinks that the reader might not have experience with which of the supplies?

    A A flower pot
    B A green foam block
    C A pencil
    D A green marker

Strategy	Explanation
✓ *Recognize the item type.*	This item tests understanding of conclusion. The word *likely* tells students that the answer is inferential rather than stated.
✓ *Use information in the item as a clue to important information in the passage.*	The words "The author likely thinks that" and "might not have experience with" indicate the author probably provides extra information to help readers overcome a lack of experience with one of the supplies. Students should mark where information is presented about each of the supplies: A A flower pot (steps 2, 3, 5, and 7) B A green foam block (steps 1–6) C A pencil (step 3) D A green marker (step 6) Then students can search those steps for extra, important information about one of the supplies. (Students can also use prior knowledge to know that options C and D are not viable since all readers probably have experience with these.)
✓ *Build a case.*	In step 1, the author describes what a green foam block is ("a special material") and tells where a green foam block can be purchased ("at an art supply store" and "your local flower shop"). Students can infer that the author thinks readers might not know what this is or where it can be found. No such extra information is presented in the steps for the supplies in options B, C, and D.

Correct answer: B. Tracking and analyzing the information that the author *does* say helps lead students to know what the author implies. By trying to build a case for each option, students should recognize that only the inference in option B can be supported.

3. The reader can infer that the green foam is important in the craft project because it—

    A prevents the flower pot from tipping over
    B keeps the lollipops in their proper place
    C is meant to look like grass growing in the pot
    D is the same color as the lollipop sticks

Strategy	Explanation
✓ *Recognize the item type.*	This item tests understanding of inference. The word *infer* in the item stem indicates that students must infer information rather than locate stated information.
✓ *Use information in the item as a clue to important information in the passage.*	The green foam is mentioned in steps 1–6. Students can reread these steps to search for clues about the importance of the green foam. Students might ask themselves, "What would not be possible without the green foam?"
✓ *Build a case.*	Within steps 1–6, students should search for information that supports each option: A (No evidence.) B (Supported. "Push the lollipop into the foam" tells readers that the foam holds the lollipops wherever the craft-maker places them.) C (No evidence. There is no mention of grass, nor can it be inferred that grass is an important aspect of the project.) D (No evidence. Be careful here. It is true that the foam and the colored sticks are green, probably so the lollipop arrangement will look a lot like a real flower arrangement. But the item asks about the foam's importance—its role. Without the foam, the lollipops would not stay in place. The color of the foam is not its important feature. Inference items like these always require some deep thinking.)

Correct answer: B. Tracking and rereading information about the green foam and trying to build a case for each option should help students find the best answer, option B.

4. What is the purpose of the passage?

   A   To entertain
   B   To persuade
   C   To compare
   D   To explain

Strategy	Explanation
✓ *Recognize the item type.*	This item tests understanding of author's purpose. The key word in the stem is *purpose*.
✓ *Have anchor examples.*	Students who can recall that a story entertains, that editorials and advertisements persuade, that nonfiction compares, and that nonfiction explains will be able to use their anchor examples to reveal the answer.
✓ *Ask a key question.*	Students can combine knowledge of purposes and text types to question the options: A Is the purpose to provide a fun read and tell a story? (No.) B Does the author aim to persuade readers to take action on an important issue? (No.) C Does the passage compare things? (No.) D Is the purpose to tell readers about something or how to do something? (Yes.)

Correct answer: D. By recognizing the item type, drawing on anchor examples, and asking key questions using knowledge of purposes and text types, students should decide that the purpose of the passage is to explain, making option D the correct answer.

5. What is the purpose of the numbered section of the craft project?

   A   It tells how to put together the bouquet.
   B   It lists the supplies needed to make the bouquet.
   C   It makes suggestions about where to find a bouquet.
   D   It tells what to do with the bouquet.

Strategy	Explanation
✓ *Recognize the item type.*	This item tests understanding of author's purpose. The word *purpose* in the stem identifies this item type.
✓ *Have anchor examples.*	Anchor examples allow students to compare what they know from more familiar texts to key words in the options, such as *tells, lists,* and *makes suggestions.* Students should associate lists/steps with a process for how to do something.
✓ *Ask a key question.*	Students can ask, "Which steps tell . . ." A how to put together the bouquet? (Steps 1–7) B what supplies are needed? (None) C where to find a bouquet? (None) D what to do with the bouquet? (Step 8)

Correct answer: A. Recognizing the key word in the stem (*purpose*), drawing on anchor examples, and asking a key question about the central idea in each option reveal that most steps pertain to putting together the bouquet, which is expressed in option A.

Searching for an Idea

1   Monica had been sitting at the kitchen table for more than an hour. She thought if she <u>concentrated</u>, she would come up with an idea. She had been thinking hard, and still she had not thought of anything. She sighed heavily when she looked down at the blank page in her notebook.

2   "I'm going to <u>fail</u> the fourth grade," she told her dad. Monica felt a knot twist tightly in her stomach. She was almost in tears now.

3   "What do you mean?" her dad asked.

4   Monica told her dad about her big assignment. Her class had been reading all kinds of poems. Now each student had to write a poem. It was due tomorrow.

5   "I can't write a poem. It's too hard," Monica said.

6   Usually Monica's dad was her homework helper. But this time, he seemed busy with other things. "You are good with words," her dad said. He smiled and walked away.

7   Monica couldn't believe what she heard. She often liked to have her dad's <u>guidance</u>. She thought he would want to write the poem with her.

8   Seconds later, Monica <u>burst</u> into her older brother's room. "I have to write a poem for school," Monica said. Then she had an idea. "If you write it with me, I'll do your kitchen chores tonight," she added. Monica knew her brother Ben hated to wash dishes.

9   Ben snatched Monica's notebook from her. He made a few scratches and then pitched the notebook back. He had written:

> Roses are red.
> Violets are blue.
> Get out of my room!
> I'm DONE WITH YOU!

10   Shooing her away, Ben put his headphones back in his ears. Monica should have known not to <u>bother</u> him while he was listening to his music.

11   Then she had another thought. She called her friend Sara and asked her what she was writing about.

12   "I'm writing about my aunt. She is so funny," Sara said. That didn't help Monica. Monica couldn't think of any humorous people she wanted to write about. Sara tried to help with other <u>suggestions</u>. "What about a place you've been or something you've read about?" Sara asked. Monica thanked Sara and hung up the phone. Still, nothing interested Monica.

13   A little while later, Monica's dad entered the kitchen again. "Is that poem written yet?" he asked.

14   Monica sat <u>speechless</u>. She simply held up her sheet of paper. There was still nothing on it.

15   "Why don't you come with me then," her dad said. "We'll try to find an idea on the way to the grocery store."

16   On the ride there, Monica stared out the window. She saw people talking on street corners. There were houses and tall buildings.

17   Monica could hear her teacher's words in her head: "You can write about anything." But Monica had nothing to say about the things around her.

18   Then Monica's dad drove the car up to an empty field.

19   "Why don't you write about this," Monica's dad said.

20   "About what?" Monica replied.

21   "Write about what you see," he said.

22   Monica sat still and stared ahead, pondering why her dad wanted her to look at the empty field. Monica then looked at him strangely.

23   "There's nothing happening here, Dad," she said. "There are no children playing. There are no flowers growing."

24   "Maybe that's what you should write!" he answered.

25   Monica looked out across the field again. Soon, thoughts danced in her head, and she struggled to get them all on paper quickly. "No children," she wrote first. "Nothing but dirt. No grass or flowers grow here," she wrote next. Monica's paper was soon full of details. She was starting to <u>reclaim</u> her confidence. "I think I'm ready now," she said after a few minutes.

26   That night, Monica went back to the kitchen table. She wrote for a long time. She crossed things out. She put words in. Her hand moved across the page like a talented artist's paintbrush across a canvas. She hardly noticed when Ben threw soap bubbles on her. She kept focusing on the empty field. That field was her safety net.

27   The next day, Monica couldn't wait until it was time for poetry reading. When her teacher asked for volunteers, Monica's hand shot up in a flash. Her teacher called on someone else, though. Monica had to wait. In her head, she practiced reading her poem to the class. She thought about how her teacher was right. A poem can be written about anything—even an empty field.

1. What does the word <u>suggestions</u> mean in paragraph 12?

   A   Problems
   B   Questions
   C   Ideas
   D   Reasons

2. Which words found in paragraph 1 help the reader know what <u>concentrated</u> means?

   A   *had been sitting*
   B   *had been thinking hard*
   C   *sighed heavily*
   D   *blank page*

3. Which words found in paragraph 12 are synonyms?

   A   *funny, humorous*
   B   *think, tried*
   C   *place, read*
   D   *something, interested*

4. Which word is an antonym of <u>fail</u> in paragraph 2?

   A   Miss
   B   Choose
   C   Explore
   D   Succeed

5. In paragraph 25, the word <u>reclaim</u> means to—

   A   happen without help
   B   explain before
   C   not notice
   D   have again

6. In paragraph 14, the word <u>speechless</u> means—

   A   without speaking
   B   filled with thoughts
   C   one who gives speeches
   D   having more thoughts

7. In paragraph 7, the root word in <u>guidance</u> means—

   A   to look for something
   B   to offer help
   C   to keep a secret
   D   to get easily

8. Read the dictionary entry below.

   burst [burst] *v.* 1. to explode or break apart
   2. to be very full 3. to do something suddenly
   4. to be very happy about something

   Which definition best matches how the word <u>burst</u> is used in paragraph 8?

   A   Definition 1
   B   Definition 2
   C   Definition 3
   D   Definition 4

9. Read this entry from a thesaurus.

   bother *v.* 1. toss, shake
   2. annoy, disturb
   3. (Idiom) get under one's skin
   4. (Ant.) easy, calm

   bother *n.* 1. fuss, annoyance
   2. irritation, difficulty, problem

   Read this sentence from paragraph 10.

   Monica should have known not to <u>bother</u> him while he was listening to his music.

   Which word could be used to replace the word <u>bother</u> in this sentence?

   A   Shake
   B   Calm
   C   Problem
   D   Disturb

10. Paragraph 26 is mainly about—

   A how Monica works hard on her poem

   B what Monica decides to write about in her poem

   C how Monica's brother is playful with her

   D where Monica completes her homework

11. According to the passage, why does Monica's dad ask her to go along to the grocery store?

   A He knows she will need more paper to finish her schoolwork.

   B He thinks they might find an idea for her poem on the way there.

   C He knows she is finished with all of her chores.

   D He thinks he might need her help with the groceries.

12. Which of these is the best summary of the passage?

   A When trying to do her assignment, Monica remembers that her teacher says a poem can be written about anything.

   B After struggling and seeking help, Monica is finally able to write a poem.

   C Monica's class has been reading poems, and now Monica has to write one.

   D Although Monica sees many things on the way to the store, she doesn't know what to say about them in a poem.

13.

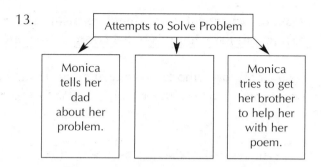

Which of these belongs in the empty box?

   A Monica volunteers in class.

   B Monica asks her teacher for help.

   C Monica tries to write about people she knows.

   D Monica calls her friend for help.

14. Monica tries to get her brother's help by offering to—

    A   go to the store for him
    B   let him listen to her music
    C   write a poem for him
    D   do his chores

15. In the passage, Monica's feelings change from—

    A   confident to regretful
    B   frustrated to satisfied
    C   unhappy to puzzled
    D   angry to nervous

16. The ending of the passage takes place—

    A   at school
    B   at a grocery store
    C   on an empty field
    D   at the kitchen table

17. What is Monica's problem in the passage?

    A   She does not think she can write a poem.
    B   She does not get along with her brother.
    C   She does not remember what her assignment is.
    D   She does not want to do her chores.

18. Which event helps Monica solve her problem?

    A   She calls her friend Sara.
    B   She tries to trade chores with her brother.
    C   She goes on an errand with her dad.
    D   She volunteers in class.

19. What is a theme of the passage?

    A   Making a change in your life can be frightening at first.
    B   Helping others is often rewarding.
    C   Don't give up trying something that is hard for you.
    D   Families teach us about ourselves.

20. In paragraph 2, the sentence "Monica felt a knot twist tightly in her stomach" means that she is—

    A   strong
    B   surprised
    C   confused
    D   worried

21. In paragraph 26, the author uses the words "like a talented artist's paintbrush across a canvas" to show that Monica—

    A   daydreams about taking art classes
    B   is a better artist than a writer
    C   wants to add an illustration to her poem
    D   is creating something beautiful

22. In paragraph 26, the metaphor "That field was her safety net" is used to show that—

    A   seeing the field makes Monica not care about her troubles
    B   Monica thinks she should write her poem about a safety net
    C   writing about the field means that Monica can complete her assignment
    D   Monica is reminded of a safety net when she sees the field

23. Read this sentence from paragraph 2.

    "I'm going to fail the fourth grade," she told her dad.

    In this sentence, the author uses—

    A   a metaphor
    B   hyperbole
    C   a simile
    D   rhyme

24. Which of these is an example of personification?

    A   *thoughts danced in her head*
    B   *dad drove the car*
    C   *she practiced reading*
    D   *she had another thought*

25. Read this sentence from paragraph 22.

    Monica sat still and stared ahead, pondering why her dad wanted her to look at the empty field.

    Which words are an example of alliteration?

    A   *sat still and stared*
    B   *pondering why*
    C   *wanted her to look*
    D   *at the empty field*

26. Monica is able to find a subject for her poem because—

   A   she remembers what her teacher tells her
   B   her dad takes her on an errand
   C   her brother writes a poem for her
   D   she wants to read a poem to her class

27. What happens right after Dad tells Monica that she should write about the empty field?

   A   Monica makes notes about what she sees.
   B   Monica practices her poem in her head.
   C   Monica's brother throws soap bubbles on her.
   D   Monica remembers her teacher's advice.

28. Based on the poem that Monica's brother writes, the reader can tell that—

   A   he is not a good student in English class
   B   he is not serious about trying to help his sister
   C   he is sharing his favorite poem with his sister
   D   he is letting her use a poem that he wrote for school

29. Which of these will likely happen next?

   A   Monica will receive an award from her teacher.
   B   Monica will plant grass and flowers in the empty field.
   C   Monica will enjoy sharing her poem with the class.
   D   Monica will rewrite her poem.

30. Which of these is an opinion in the passage?

   A   *Monica told her dad about her big assignment.*
   B   *"I have to write a poem for school," Monica said.*
   C   *Monica looked out across the field again.*
   D   *"You are good with words," her dad said.*

31. Which sentence in the last paragraph best shows how Monica feels about the poem she has written?

   A   *When her teacher asked for volunteers, Monica's hand shot up in a flash.*
   B   *In her head, she practiced reading her poem to the class.*
   C   *She thought about how her teacher was right.*
   D   *A poem can be written about anything—even an empty field.*

32. What is the purpose of the passage?

 A To persuade
 B To inform
 C To entertain
 D To describe

33. The passage can best be described as—

 A mystery
 B tall tale
 C biography
 D realistic fiction

34. How is the passage mostly organized?

 A Comparison and contrast
 B Problem and solution
 C Cause and effect
 D Step-by-step instructions

Demonstrating Understandings with Reading Activities

This section is designed with the principle that students need opportunities to demonstrate what they know and develop new understandings as strategic readers and thinkers, and that teachers need opportunities to introduce, review, and reteach reading skills and to assess what students know in order to build on their understandings.

The thirty-plus activities (and various resources pages) that compose this section are based on the most commonly assessed reading standards. Each activity includes some or all of these parts:

- an introduction or purpose statement
- a list of resources needed
- a set of procedures
- a model
- an assessment
- an extension
- student samples

The activities are print-rich. They are easy for teachers to prepare for because they require only a few, easily accessed materials. The procedures are simple for teachers to follow and allow for flexibility. The assessments allow students to reflect on their thinking, their challenges, and their successes. Through these assessments, teachers can gain entrance to the students' thinking and can celebrate lightbulb moments and can clarify and expand on lesser-formed ideas (Serafini 2004). Students are invited to work collaboratively to construct meaning (Vygotsky 1978), to think creatively, to problem-solve, and to feel confident as learners.

159

The activities are also designed to fit in with the gradual release of responsibility model of instruction (Pearson and Gallagher 1983). That is, some activities will work well as introductions to reading skills, with the teacher introducing and defining terms and concepts and modeling the tasks. Other activities include only a short guided practice, because the standards involved are more familiar to students. That way, the majority of the time is spent allowing students to practice their skills with little teacher oversight; these activities are fairly open, allowing students to draw on other reading comprehension strategies that teachers have taught (such as the excellent strategies presented in *Strategies That Work* [Harvey and Goudvis 2007]). Still other activities are planned specifically for the purpose of equipping students with strategies that they can access during reading assessments—such as building anchor examples and other tools that students can personalize for their use. No matter how teachers decide to incorporate these activities into their reading instruction, they are meant to be inviting, varied, interactive, thought provoking, and confidence boosting.

Contents

Activities for Vocabulary Development

Activities for Important Ideas

Activities for Literary Elements

Activities for Literary Techniques

Activities for Interpretations

This Leads to That   (Cause-Effect)
"I Am" Inferences   (Conclusion/Inference)
School Facts and Opinions   (Fact/Opinion)
Sentence Search   (Supporting Evidence)

Activities for Text Matters

What's the Purpose?   (Author's Purpose)
You Name It!   (Text Type)
Putting Together How Ideas Are
      Put Together   (Author's Organization)

Activities for Vocabulary Development

Context Clues

Poetic Words

Reading poems with students chorally is a great way to get them thinking about word meaning, because poets often make painstaking decisions about rhythm and word choice. Students might be surprised that they can employ context clue strategies even with short texts like poems.

Resources

Poetry book: Prelutsky, Jack. 1990. *Something Big Has Been Here.* New York: Greenwillow Books.
Overhead projector and transparency of poem
Chart paper and marker

Procedure and Assessment

Prepare by reading the poems "I Met a Rat of Culture" and "My Mother Made a Meatloaf" from Jack Prelutsky's book *Something Big Has Been Here.* (These poems should contain several words that are unfamiliar to students.) Choose one poem and make a transparency of it.

Share the poem a few times—with you reading the poem aloud the first time as students follow along on a transparency, and then with the students reading the poem chorally.

Make an anchor chart of the types and examples of context clues found in Chapter 3 on page 30. Using the teacher's guide found at the end of this activity, lead a discussion by pointing out focus words one by one and asking students to share how they can use context clues to help them understand these words. Refer to the types/examples of context clues as needed and review other strategies for determining the meanings of unfamiliar words.

Teacher's Guide

POEM "I MET A RAT OF CULTURE"

Possible Focus Words:	Clues:
culture	Clued through description throughout the poem
elegantly	Clued through description of clothes (*velvet*, etc.)
shed light	Clue word *instructed*
circled	Clue word *visited*
operetta	Clued through definition (a type of song)
gavotte	Clued through definition (a type of dance)
versed	Clue word *authority*; clue words *within his brains*; antonym clue words *did not know*
rodent	Clue word *rat* in the title and the last line
sonata	Clued through description (music played on a violin); clue word *performed*

POEM "MY MOTHER MADE A MEATLOAF"

Possible Focus Words:	Clues:
distress	Clued through description; clue words *no success*
powerless	Clue words *no success*
assailed	Clue words *whacked* and *smacked*
impression	Clue words *without a nick*
chisel	Clued through description/definition (something that *chips* or *dents*)
unblemished	Clued through description; clue words *didn't make a dent*
beset	Clued through parts of speech: other verbs mean *attack*
manufacture	Clued through parts of speech: verb *building*
Synonyms for *failure* throughout poem	*met with no success, powerless, failed completely to suffice, couldn't faze, made no impression, didn't make a dent, stayed unblemished, didn't make a difference, simply stood its ground*
Use of verbs to describe attempts to cut	*whacked, smacked, assailed, worked, chipped, set upon, fired at, beset, trample*

Antonyms

That's an Antonym

Resources

Picture books (see suggestions that follow)
Antonym words (suggestions provided in the appendix)
Chalkboard or whiteboard
Paper and drawing supplies

Suggested Picture Books

Charlip, Remy. 1993. *Fortunately*. New York: Aladdin.
Cleary, Brian. P. 2006. *Stop and Go, Yes and No: What Is an Antonym?*
    Minneapolis: Carolrhoda Books.
Cuyler, Margery. 1993. *That's Good! That's Bad!* New York: Henry Holt.
———. 2002. *That's Good! That's Bad! in the Grand Canyon.* New York:
    Henry Holt.
———. 2007. *That's Good! That's Bad! in Washington, DC.* New York:
    Henry Holt.

Procedure

Read Cuyler's *That's Good! That's Bad!* aloud to the class. Draw attention to the examples of good and bad by discussing how they represent antonyms. (If students need more examples of antonyms, select another suggested picture book and read it aloud.)

Place students in small groups. Then give each group a pair of words that are antonyms. (If desired, use the antonyms provided for the activity "Charades, Double Time" on pages 168–169.)

Tell students to write and draw an example of the antonym words you provide. Work through the model as described below to show students how to complete this task.

Model

On the board, draw the outline of a piece of paper and split it in half horizontally. On the top half, write the words "Someone lost in the desert in the blazing sun," and directly below it, write "That's hot!" On the bottom half, write the words "Someone playing outside in the snow wearing only a T-shirt and shorts," and directly below it, write "That's cold!"

Have volunteers come to the board to illustrate the descriptions. As they do, allow other students to talk about why the descriptions you have written are examples of the antonyms hot and cold.

Tell students that they will work in their groups to think of an image that represents each of the words you provide them. Remind students of the process: Divide a sheet of paper in half; think of an image to represent the word; write descriptive words; write "That's [fill in antonym word]" under the descriptive words; make an illustration.

Assessment   When groups are finished working, allow them to share their work. Prompt students to talk about how they thought of their descriptions and illustrations, and focus on how these words are antonyms.

Student Samples   Third graders, following a read-aloud of Cuyler's (1993) *That's Good! That's Bad!*, demonstrate what they know about antonyms. See the figures that follow.

FIGURE 1 Brooke and Cody illustrate the difference between feeling *calm* and being *nervous*.

FIGURE 2 Thea and Chelsea know that *clean* is an antonym of *dirty*.

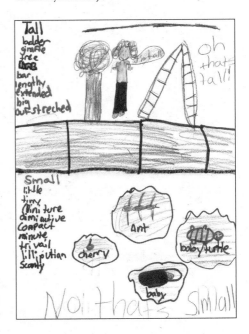

FIGURE 3 Starr provides synonyms and multiple examples of the opposites *tall* and *small*.

Antonyms

Opposites Attract

Resources

Copier and paper

"Antonym Squares," including answer key (provided in the appendix)

Procedure

Prepare by copying the "Antonym Squares" sheet (provided in the appendix) so that each student gets one.

Ask students to work in groups to discuss which word is an antonym of the word that is in bold at the top of each square. Have students circle their choice. Model the task, if needed.

Model

Explain that the students should decide the meaning of the bolded word *guilty* in the first square and then search for its opposite. Point out that *guilty* and *innocent* are antonyms. Tell students that they should circle *innocent*.

Assessment

While students are working, circulate to listen in on and add to the conversations.

When all groups are finished, use the answer key to discuss the groups' responses to each square.

Remediation/Extension

The words used on the antonym squares are words that students might be expected to identify as character traits on a reading assessment. (See page 196 for a list of character traits.) So, in addition to assessing the students' ability to recognize antonyms, this activity should provide insight into the character traits that they recognize without the need of a context. Those traits that are unfamiliar to students can be taught with texts that are available in the classroom or library as well as with the activities about character that appear later in this section.

Synonyms/Antonyms

Charades, Double Time

Resources

Synonym/Antonym Cards (provided in the appendix)

Copier and paper

Scissors

Chalkboard or whiteboard

Procedure　　Prepare by deciding if the class will work with synonyms or antonyms. Make one copy of the "Synonym/Antonym Cards" sheet (provided in the appendix) and cut them apart with scissors.

Place students in pairs. Ask a pair of students to come to the front of the room. Give the students one card. Instruct one student to act out one of the words and the other student to act out the other word—both at the same time!

Tell the other pairs of students to guess the words being acted out. When one of the words is correctly identified, stop the action. Write the word on the board, and reward that pair with one point by keeping score on the board. Then restart the game, with the student continuing to act out the remaining word. When that second word is identified, award one point to whichever pair guesses it.

Proceed in this fashion until all pairs of students have had a round at the front of the room.

Extension　　Have groups create their own synonym or antonym cards to continue the game. Or make synonym or antonyms cards from a current unit of study or the character traits list found on page 196.

Prefixes, Roots/Base Words, Suffixes

The Breakup

Segmenting words to identify prefixes, roots/base words, and suffixes is a strategy that students can use on a reading assessment when approaching unfamiliar words that assess word parts.

Resources　　Copier and paper
Scissors
"Breakup Cards" (provided in the appendix)
Chalkboard or whiteboard

Procedure　　Prepare by copying and cutting apart four sets of breakup cards from the sheets provided in the appendix. Cut out each box so that the words are separated from their meanings.

Divide the class into four groups.

Ask students to work together to segment each of the words by drawing a line between the word's parts. Provide an example by writing "unacceptable" on the board and asking a volunteer to divide the word into three parts: un / accept / able.

Also ask groups to match the word card with the corresponding meaning card by using their knowledge of prefixes, roots/base words, and suffixes.

Assessment   Ask groups to compare their matches. Monitor the discussion and focus on how the recognizable word parts contribute to the meanings of the words.

Extension   Throughout the year, draw attention to and collect other words that have recognizable segments. Repeat this activity when a sufficient number of new words have been collected.

Multiple-Meaning Words

A New Twist on Hangman

Resources   List of multiple-meaning words and definitions (provided at the end of this activity)
Chalkboard or whiteboard

Procedure   Prepare by selecting from the list provided multiple-meaning words for which students likely know at least one of the definitions.
Divide students into small teams.
Begin by putting blanks on the board for every letter of the first word, as is done in the game hangman. Fill in one letter. Then read aloud one definition for the word. Ask the first team to make a guess. If the team guesses the word correctly, it scores a point. If not, fill in another letter and read aloud another definition. Allow the second team to guess. Continue in this way until the word is guessed correctly and a team scores a point. Keep score on the board. For each new word, start with a different team so that each team gets the same number of chances to go first.
If all definitions are read before a team guesses the word and before all letters are filled in, add the remaining letters. Teach the word and meanings by giving examples or by providing students with print or online dictionaries that provide examples that they can read aloud and discuss.

Sample of Procedure   The game might proceed in the following way for the word *dash*:

Add letter: _ <u>A</u> _ _ → Read "to move quickly."   → Team guesses incorrectly.
Add letter: _ <u>A</u> _ <u>H</u> → Read "to break to pieces."   → Team guesses incorrectly.
Add letter: <u>D</u> <u>A</u> _ <u>H</u> → Read "a punctuation mark." → Team guesses correctly.
Fill in the last letter and read the last definition. Discuss the word and meanings.

Extension   Continue the study of the multiple-meaning words used in the game by creating and playing other word games such as memory, charades, or Pictionary.

MULTIPLE-MEANING WORDS AND DEFINITIONS

DASH 1 (v) to move quickly 2 (v) to break to pieces 3 (n) a punctuation mark 4 (n) a small amount	**MODEL** 1 (n) a person who is a good example 2 (n) someone who poses for a photographer 3 (adj) small or miniature in size	**DEGREE** 1 (n) a unit for measuring temperature 2 (n) an award given out by a college or university 3 (n) a step in a series
RARE 1 (adj) lightly cooked 2 (adj) not happening or seen often 3 (adj) unusually good or excellent at something	**ORDER** 1 (v) to command 2 (v) to ask for something in a restaurant 3 (n) neatness or cleanliness 4 (n) a particular sequence	**STRIKE** 1 (v) to make an impression on someone 2 (v) to hit or attack 3 (v) to refuse to work 4 (n) a call made by an umpire in a baseball game
TRAIN 1 (v) to prepare by practicing 2 (n) the long piece of fabric behind a bride's dress 3 (n) a string of railroad cars	**LAST** 1 (v) to go on for a particular amount of time 2 (v) to stay in good condition for a particular amount of time 3 (adj) being the only one left	**ALARM** 1 (v) to make someone afraid that something bad might happen 2 (n) a device that warns of danger 3 (n) a ringer meant to wake people up
FRAME 1 (n) the way a person's body is built 2 (v) to make it look like an innocent person is guilty 3 (n) a border that surrounds something, such as a picture	**COVER** 1 (v) to travel a certain distance 2 (v) to study a certain topic well 3 (v) to put something over something else	**PICTURE** 1 (v) to describe something in words 2 (v) to imagine something 3 (n) a movie 4 (n) an image, such as a painting or drawing
ADDRESS 1 (v) to deal with something, such as a problem 2 (v) to give a speech to an audience 3 (n) the street name and number of a place	**CHECK** 1 (v) to look at something to make sure it's right 2 (n) a mark used to show that a thing has been looked at 3 (n) a piece of paper used by people and banks	**PLACE** 1 (v) to put something somewhere 2 (n) a space for a person or thing 3 (n) a particular area or location
CROSS 1 (adj) angry or not pleased 2 (v) to go from one side to another 3 (v) to draw a line through something	**STAGE** 1 (v) to organize a public performance 2 (n) a level of progress or accomplishment 3 (n) a platform on which actors perform	**RATTLE** 1 (v) to make a rapid series of short or sharp noises 2 (v) to talk or say something quickly 3 (n) a baby's toy that makes sound
SKIP 1 (v) to move along in a bouncy way 2 (v) to leave something out or pass over 3 (v) to go past one grade in school by going to the next one	**SHOCK** 1 (n) the effect of an electric current 2 (n) a sudden and violent event 3 (n) the feeling caused by a sudden and violent event	**NATURAL** 1 (n) a person who is good at something 2 (adj) normal or usual 3 (adj) found or produced in nature
RACE 1 (n) a test of speed 2 (v) to run or move quickly 3 (n) a group into which human beings are divided	**PLAY** 1 (v) to take part in a game 2 (n) a story that is acted out 3 (v) to make music on	**EXPRESS** 1 (adj) very fast 2 (v) to show what you feel 3 (n) a fast train or bus

Vocabulary Building

Word Costumes

Resources   Picture book: Frasier, Debra. 2000. *Miss Alaineus: A Vocabulary Disaster.*
Orlando: Harcourt.
Paper and drawing supplies
Dictionaries
Bookbinding supplies

Procedure   Read Frasier's picture book, *Miss Alaineus: A Vocabulary Disaster*, to students. Throughout the read-aloud, draw attention to the highlighted words.

On the last few pages of the book are illustrations of the "Vocabulary Parade" that Sage's class puts on in the school auditorium. Discuss each word costume. Focus on the aspects of the costumes that express each word's meaning(s).

Re-create the concept of a vocabulary parade: Have each student select a vocabulary word from the picture book or from a unit of study or other activity the students are completing presently. Tell each student to use paper and drawing supplies to design a costume for the selected word and create an illustration of someone wearing it. Provide students access to the picture book, and remind students that the costume should represent the word's meaning(s). Ask students to write the word and its dictionary definition(s) at the bottom of their drawing.

Assessment   Give students the opportunity to present their illustrations to the class and explain the aspects that relate to the word's meaning(s). After each student shares, call on three or more student volunteers to offer compliments. (Suggest that compliments begin "I like how . . .")

Extension   Create a class book of the word costumes using bookbinding supplies. Throughout the year, as students finish units of study or other activities that focus on groups of words, ask students to create additional word costumes for the class book.

Student Samples   Third graders create word costumes using words that they are presently studying in science and social studies. See the figures that follow.

FIGURE 4   Cheyanne designs a costume for the word *feast* and very creatively finds many areas to place food—including on the top of the head!

FIGURE 5   Brooks's costumed person is magnetic! He can attract iron and steel, as is indicated in the definition of *magnet*.

FIGURE 6   Josh's illustration places a person squarely in the desert, and a *reptile* is featured prominently in the middle of the costume.

Suggested Picture Books About Vocabulary Topics

Parts of Speech

Barrett, Judi. 2001. *Things That Are Most in the World.* New York: Aladdin.

Cleary, Brian P. 1999. *A Mink, a Fink, a Skating Rink: What Is a Noun?* Minneapolis: Carolrhoda Books.

———. 2000. *Hairy, Scary, Ordinary: What Is an Adjective?* Minneapolis: Carolrhoda Books.

———. 2001. *To Root, to Shoot, to Parachute: What Is a Verb?* Minneapolis: Carolrhoda Books.

———. 2002. *Under, Over, By the Clover: What Is a Preposition?* Minneapolis: Carolrhoda Books.

———. 2003. *Dearly, Nearly, Insincerely: What Is an Adverb?* Minneapolis: Carolrhoda Books.

———. 2004. *I and You and Don't Forget Who: What Is a Pronoun?* Minneapolis: Carolrhoda Books.

———. 2006a. *A Lime, a Mime, a Pool of Slime: More About Nouns.* Minneapolis: Carolrhoda Books.

———. 2006b . *Slide and Slurp, Scratch and Burp: More About Verbs.* Minneapolis: Carolrhoda Books.

———. 2007. *Quirky, Jerky, Extra Perky: More About Adjectives.* Minneapolis: Carolrhoda Books.

Heller, Ruth. 1995. *Behind the Mask: A Book About Prepositions.* New York: Putnam.

———. 1998a. *A Cache of Jewels and Other Collective Nouns.* New York: Putnam.

———. 1998b. *Kites Sail Higher: A Book About Verbs.* New York: Putnam.

———. 1998c. *Many Luscious Lollipops: A Book About Adjectives.* New York: Putnam.

———. 1998d. *Merry-Go-Round: A Book About Nouns.* New York: Putnam.

———. 1998e. *Up, Up and Away: A Book About Adverbs.* New York: Putnam.

———. 1999. *Mine, All Mine: A Book About Pronouns.* New York: Putnam.

Pulver, Robin. 2006. *Nouns and Verbs Have a Field Day.* New York: Holiday House.

Walton, Rick. 2004. *Suddenly Alligator: An Adverbial Tale.* Salt Lake City: Gibbs Smith.

———. 2006. *Around the House the Fox Chased the Mouse: A Prepositional Tale.* Salt Lake City: Gibbs Smith.

Synonyms

Cleary, Brian P. 2004. *Pitch and Throw, Grasp and Know: What Is a Synonym?* Minneapolis: Carolrhoda Books.

Words Parts

Most, Bernard. 1992. *There's an Ant in Anthony.* New York: HarperTrophy.
Walton, Rick. 2005. *Once There Was a Bull . . . Frog.* Salt Lake City: Gibbs
Smith.

Multiple-Meaning Words

Grover, Max. 1997. *Max's Wacky Taxi Day.* Orlando: Harcourt.
Parish, Peggy. Amelia Bedelia series. New York: HarperTrophy.
Walton, Rick. 2005. *Bullfrog Pops.* Salt Lake City: Gibbs Smith.

Using a Thesaurus

Walton, Rick. 2005. *Why the Banana Split.* Salt Lake City: Gibbs Smith.

PREFIXES, SUFFIXES, AND ROOTS FOR ELEMENTARY STUDENTS

Prefix	Definition	Example(s)
dis-	opposite, not, not having	dissatisfied
extra-	beyond, more than	extracurricular, extraordinary
im-, in-, ir-	not	impatient, inactive, irregular
in-	into, inside of, toward	inhale, inspire
mis-	wrongly, incorrectly	misguide, misinform
non-	not	nonsense
over-	too much	overflow
pre-	before, early in time	premature, preview
re-	again	review
un-	not	uncomfortable
un-	reverse	untie
sub-	under	submarine

Suffix	Definition	Example(s)
-able, -ible	able to, able to have, having	comfortable, flexible
-ance	action, state, or process	appearance, performance
-ar, -er, -ist, -or	one who does	beggar, farmer, violinist, actor
-en	make or made of	frozen, wooden
-er	more	quicker
-ion, -sion, -tion	state, action, or results of	decoration, permission, elimination
-ity, -ty	quality or state of	creativity, sensitivity
-ive	having, making, showing	creative
-ial, -ize	to make (making), to do	memorial, summarize
-ful	full of, having	successful
-less	without, having none	harmless, useless
-logy	study of	biology
-ly	in the manner of	softly
-ment	process, result, or act of	announcement, excitement
-ness	quality or act	kindness
-ous	having	dangerous, jealous
-y	having	greedy, sleepy

Root	Definition	Example(s)
aud	hear	audience, audio
bio	life	biology, biography
chrono	time	chronicle, chronology
fract, frag	break	fraction, fragment
geo	earth	geographic, geothermal
gram	something written	telegram
graph	writing	autograph
grat	pleasing	congratulations, grateful
hab, habit	live, have	habit, habitat
magn	great	magnify, magnitude
mem	remember	memory, memoir, memorial
phon	sound	phonograph, symphony
port	carry	portable, support
scrib, script	write	describe, inscribe, prescription
sens	feel	sensation, sensitive
spect	look	inspect, spectacle
tele	far, distance	telephone, telescope
val	value, worth	evaluation, valid, valor
vid, vis	see	vivid, invisible

Activities for Important Ideas

Main Ideas/Comprehension

Chunk, Sum, and Picture

Passages on reading assessments can be quite long. Because students need to refer back to them in order to answer the items, they need a way to remember where certain major events or topics are located; otherwise, they might end up reading the entire passage again and again. Using the strategy of "chunk, sum, and picture" as explained in detail in Chapter 4, students can learn to divide text into manageable chunks, summarize important events with key words, and/or use pictures or expressive faces to remember important moments in the passage—all of which can be helpful when students refer back to the passage later to track down an answer.

Resources
"Story Windows" (provided in the appendix)
Copier and paper
Picture book: Mora, Pat. 1997. *Tomas and the Library Lady*. New York: Alfred A. Knopf.
Markers
Chalkboard or whiteboard

Procedure
Prepare by making one copy of the "Story Windows" sheet (provided in the appendix) for each student.

Tell students that as you read *Tomas and the Library Lady*, you will stop along the way and ask them to write a key word or phrase and/or draw a picture to express what is happening. Tell students that they can also use a "feeling face" to express how the main character is feeling in the story. (If desired, allow students to work in pairs or small groups.)

Distribute a copy of "Story Windows" sheet and markers to each student.

Begin reading. After the first or second page, stop to model on the board an example of what students might place in their first story window. Draw an outline of the state of Texas and/or a car and write the words "Tomas leaves Texas."

Continue reading. Stop at the end of each page; for pages with a great deal of text, stop a few times, if desired. Continue to model or discuss what students could place in their story windows. Throughout, keep a quick pace; spending too much time on any one story window could interfere with the students' ability to stay with the text.

After the first reading, begin reading the story a second time, pausing in the same places and allowing students to share what they have drawn and written in their story windows to help them remember that chunk of text.

Assessment
When students first use the strategy, they may take too much time thinking about what to write and draw, which ultimately might hinder comprehen-

sion. Some students might want to include too many ideas; some might write words or phrases that are too vague or unimportant. Listen to the responses as students share their story windows to gauge their understanding of the strategy and recognize the purpose and usefulness of it. With practice using a wide variety of texts, students should become accustomed to the technique and it should aid their comprehension. Then you can show students how to re-create their story windows within the margins of a test passage.

Because the goal of the strategy is to help students locate important text to answer test items easily, enrich the discussion by asking important questions about the story and determining if students can read their story windows to recall significant events. As students answer the questions, have them show and discuss which of their story windows helped them to remember. Doing so will further help students see the value of the strategy.

Student Sample   Fourth graders David and Brady, with lively collaboration and a bit of compromise, choose key words and add illustrations to complete their story windows during a reading of *Tomas and the Library Lady*. See the figure that follows.

FIGURE 7

Details

Quick Find

Detail items should be the easiest type of item for students, because the answers are explicitly stated or paraphrased in the passage. Still, students need strategies for navigating the passage so that they can track down the answer. In this activity, students will locate details by using text organizers (such as subheadings) and text features (such as sidebars, maps, and photos with captions); students can also use other strategies they have been taught, such as underlining key words and making drawings (see previous activity, "Chunk, Sum, and Picture") to locate important information.

Resources   Classroom magazines or textbooks with informational articles
Copier and paper
Chalkboard or whiteboard

Procedure   Prepare by finding an informational article that has several subheadings and other text features. Make a copy of the article for each student. Read the article and highlight important details. Then formulate simple questions so that the answers are the details you have highlighted.

Place students in small groups. Distribute a copy of the article, not highlighted or marked in any way, to each student.

Proceed by posing the detail questions, one by one, that you have prepared. Instruct each group to find the information as quickly as possible. Award one point to the team of the group member who answers the question first. Keep score on the board.

After each question, ask the student with the answer to reveal his or her strategy for finding the answer. Emphasize how key words in the question can be matched to key words in the text organizers and text features to help students know where to go to find the correct answer.

Extension   Photocopy additional informational articles from various sources. Ask groups to find details that can be used to formulate questions.

Then have groups exchange their articles and questions. Groups should work together to find the answers to the detail questions formulated by other groups. Encourage discussion of their strategies for locating information.

Summary

Pass It On

Students summarize all the time. They answer questions like "How was your day?", "What was the movie about?", and What did you do at the party?" This activity draws attention to the fact that students summarize without giving the process much thought. In a fun way, the activity causes students to think about the process of summarization—narrowing information into smaller, condensed ideas—so that they're more mindful of it when they encounter a summary item on a reading assessment.

Resources
"Story Cards" (provided in the appendix)
Copier and paper
Scissors
Overhead projector and transparency of the "Story Cards" sheet
Audio recording device
Chalkboard or whiteboard

Procedure
Make one copy of the "Story Cards" sheet (provided in the appendix) and cut out the stories so that there are five. Also make a transparency of the "Story Cards" sheet.

Arrange five seats at the front of the room in a line. Have five volunteers come up and take these seats so that they are facing the class.

Announce that the students will be playing a version of the game called "telephone." Give a story card to a student at one end of the row. Ask this first student to read the story card by whispering into the second student's ear. When finished, ask the second student to whisper what was said to the third student. (Only the first student has seen the printed words.) Continue in this way until the last student is told the story.

Then have the last student say out loud what he or she remembers of the story. If possible, audio-record what this last student says. Write the student's recollection on the board.

Show a transparency of the story cards, covering up all the cards except the one that is being discussed by the last student.

Ask students in the class to compare the two responses—the original version on the transparency and the last student's version on the board. (Students might find humor in how some information has changed after it has been retold down the line of students.) Use the following guiding questions for your discussion:

- What information is the same? (Most of it, some of it, hardly any of it?)
- What has been reworded or is missing? (Major ideas or minor details?)

Focus on the fact that as information is passed from one person to another, the exact wording is forgotten. Instead, the students start to summarize the information by repeating the main ideas and most important details; minor details are left out. Remind students that this is how a summary is formulated—by focusing on the main ideas and most important details.

Proceed to the next story card, allowing five different volunteers to participate. Follow the same procedure.

Summary

Summarization All Around

Summarizing can be difficult skill for readers of any age. Learning to emphasize major points while also deemphasizing minor details is easier over time—and with practice. Practicing the skill of summarization can be made more interesting by attempting to summarize a wide variety of print sources—especially those that a student wouldn't think to summarize, like the content on the back of a cereal box or a comic strip.

Resources   Various print sources (see suggestions in Procedure section)
Paper and pens

Procedure   Prepare by collecting four print sources of different types. Suggestions include an Aesop fable, the back of a cereal box, a one-page magazine advertisement with pictures and prose, and a comic strip.

Divide students into four groups.

Distribute one print source to each group. Tell groups that they are to read the print source and write a summary of it.

At this point, either review summary-writing strategies that have been previously taught and/or introduce new strategies and allow students to select which is most relevant to writing a summary of their print source. (Strategies might include writing a summary with only a certain number of words or sentences; using two columns—one marked "keep" and one marked "toss"—and deciding which events/details/ideas should be collected under each column; and using the five W's of journalism.)

When all groups are finished, have the groups trade the print sources. Continue in this fashion until every group has written a summary for each print source.

Assessment   Have groups share their summaries for a particular print source. Lead a discussion about the similar and different aspects of each summary.

Draw attention to the key aspects of producing a summary by allowing students to determine whether all the major points are included in some way and whether minor details are avoided. Discuss the strategies that each group used and decide on the effectiveness of some strategies versus others for summarizing particular kinds of print.

Extension   Throughout the year, reinforce the skill of summarization by prompting students to summarize nontext sources as well. Some suggestions are the principal's announcement over the loudspeaker; a bus ride to school; the teacher's explanation of a new assignment/project; and the goings-on at recess, the school carnival, or a baseball game.

Activities for Literary Elements

Character

Similar Traits

Resources   Copier and paper
"Pick Three" sheet, including answer key (provided in the appendix)
Pens
"Character Traits" list (provided in the appendix)

Procedure   Prepare by making one copy of the "Pick Three" sheet (provided in the appendix) for each student.

Place students in pairs. Instruct students to determine which three character traits have a similar meaning to the trait in bold print at the top of each box. Ask students to cross out the word that does not belong with the others.

Model   To provide an example, explain that in the first box, students should search for the three character traits that are similar to the trait *afraid*. Point out that *frightened, scared,* and *fearful* are character traits that are similar in meaning to *afraid*, but that *bold* is not and should be crossed out.

Assessment   As students are working, circulate to listen in on and add to the conversations. When all students are finished, use the answer key to discuss their responses.

Extension   This activity should provide insight into the character traits that students recognize without the need of a context. Those traits that are unfamiliar to students can be taught with texts that are available in the classroom or library.

For additional practice and/or to further diagnose students' awareness of character traits that are commonly tested on state assessments, have each group make new "Pick Three" sheets using the "Character Traits" list in the appendix. Ask groups to trade their new sheets with other groups, complete the sheets, and discuss their responses with the groups that created them.

Character/Plot

How Was Your Day?

Resources   "Character Traits" list (provided in the appendix)
Overhead projector and transparencies (described below)
Drawing supplies
Bookbinding supplies

Procedure   Place students in small groups.

Assign each group a character trait from the "Character Traits" list found in the appendix. (Select a recently studied trait or one with which you think students might be familiar.)

Place the following information on a transparency and show it to the class:

My name is _____ *(character trait).*
Today was a _____ *day.*
Getting ready for school today, _____.
At recess, _____.
At lunch, _____.
During _____ *class,* _____.
That is what life is like when you're _____ *(character trait).*

Tell students to think of the character trait as a person and decide how that person might feel in a particular situation or setting. Provide the model shown below. Then allow groups to use drawing supplies to complete the task for the trait assigned to them.

Model   Write this example on a transparency and discuss:

My name is Upset.
Today was a terrible day.
Getting ready for school today, I realized that I hadn't told my mom that I needed to wear my school shirt. It was dirty so I couldn't wear it.
At recess, my football team lost because I fumbled the ball.
At lunch, my friend David squirted ketchup all over me.
During science class, I knocked over our ant aquarium. There must have been a million ants going in all directions.
That is what life is like when you're Upset.

Assessment   As groups are working, circulate to listen in on and contribute to the discussion. If students need more information about their character trait, encourage them to look up the trait in the dictionary or remind them of a recently read story that relates to the trait.

When all groups are finished, allow them to share what they have written about their trait.

Extension   Use bookbinding supplies to create a class book of the groups' work.

Ask students to create additional pages when books that are read and discussed as a class present opportunities to learn about character traits that are unfamiliar to students.

Student Samples   Fourth and fifth graders know just how feeling words feel. See the figures that follow.

FIGURE 8 Kevin's trait, *Frustrated,* can't catch a break!

FRUSTRATED

My name is frustrated.
Today was a mad day.
Getting ready for school today, I did not talk to anyone while eating breakfast.
At recess, I yelled at all my friends and told everybody to be quiet.
At lunch, I couldn't eat my lunch because it was some chaos.
During spelling class, I could not spell any word because my pencil broke and when I came back from sharpening it was over.
 That is what life is like when you're frustrated.

Andrew

My name is Rambunctious.
Today was a good day!
Getting ready for school today, I slurped down my cereal and didn't chew with my mouth closed. I also threw my pajamas down the stairs. My mom had to clean it all up. This is the kind of havoc I live on.
At recess I threw mud at some kindergarteners, plowed the soccer team's faces into the ground, and threw some people's basketballs into the street.
At lunch, I told the lunch ladies their food stinks, and ate everyone else's food.
In science class I threw all the frogs we were dissecting all over the floor. I also made a chemical combination in chemistry that made the school blow up.
This is what life's like when you're Rambunctious!

FIGURE 9 Andrew's trait, *Rambunctious,* wreaks havoc throughout the day.

How Was Your Day?
By: Kendall

My name is Daring.
Today was an awesome day.
Getting ready for school today, my clothes were in my closet and my closet was slipshod so I'd have to venture into the dark chamber facing horrible scum monsters and dreadful sock zombies.
At recess, I traveled threw the mysterious depths of the jungle gym, dodging bugs, spiders and basketballs.
At lunch, I made an attempt to try the lunch ladies mystery meat pot pie… and then threw up for five minutes.
During science class, I made the first incision into the dead frog for dissection, and half the class threw up.
That is what life's like when you're Daring.

FIGURE 10 Kendall's trait, *Daring,* among other adventures, conquers the cafeteria's mystery meat—but not without a consequence!

Character

A Feeling Kind of Day

Resources   Picture book: Curtis, Jaime L. 1998. *Today I Feel Silly and Other Moods That Make My Day*. New York: HarperCollins.
Chalkboard or whiteboard
"Character Traits" list (provided in the appendix)
Overhead projector and transparency listing character traits (described in the Procedure section)
Drawing supplies

Procedure   Read the picture book aloud. During the reading, focus on the words that are character traits: *silly, angry, joyful, confused*, and so forth.

When finished reading, write these lines on the board:

Today I am angry.
You'd better stay clear.
My face is all pinched
and red ear to ear.

Ask students to detect the rhyme in the lines. Allow a student volunteer to answer that the last words in the second line and fourth line rhyme.

Display on a transparency some of the character traits from the list provided in the appendix. Place students in pairs; ask each pair to select a trait, or assign a trait to each pair. (Perhaps the class needs a review on some traits or is learning new traits, or maybe some traits are connected to another activity the students are working on in class.)

Provide the pairs with drawing supplies so they can create a four-line rhyming example of the trait, along with an illustration.

Assessment   Have student pairs present their four-line examples and illustrations to the class. Allow students to talk about what the trait means and how they came up with the example. As needed, provide more discussion or examples to help students develop a deep understanding of the traits' meanings.

Extension   One way to extend this activity is to ask students to help you group the traits that the class worked with and/or those on the "Character Traits" list. Place traits such as *sad, angry*, and *mad* together as well as *confused* and *puzzled* and *determined* and *hardworking*. As students provide suggestions, talk about how these traits are synonyms and provide more examples or situations that describe them. Making connections among traits will help them when they encounter characterization items on reading tests.

Another way to extend this activity is to create a character traits class book. As students learn more traits, they can create additional pages. Throughout the year, the class book can be read during students' free reading time or can be used as an introduction to another activity about character.

Student Samples   Fourth graders imagine what it's like to feel a certain way. See the figures that follow.

FIGURE 11 Adriana knows a *furious* shout when she hears one.

> today I am furious. You'd better stay away.
> My face is as red as a tomato. You will Pay!
> My mom told me to go downstairs, she shut me out!
> I want to run away. Insted I will only shout!
>
> Adriana

FIGURE 12 Leslie gets the last word on being *active*.

> Today I feel active. I want to jump and scream
> I'd like to kick and throw. I am the best on my team.
> I'll run around the field. I'll be the wildest at the park.
> To play is what I want to do. And that is my last remark.
>
> Leslie

Today I Feel Lucky

Today I feel Lucky.
I saw a shooting star.
I found $100.00 and
Bought 1,000 candy bars.

By: Travis and
Jonathan

FIGURE 13 Travis and Jonathan are *lucky*—and probably hyper.

Nervous

By: Ryann and Sharada

Today I feel nervous,
I'm going to be in a play.
I'll be the lead singer
Will I be good today?

FIGURE 14 Ryann and Sharada pose a *nervous* question.

Character

Bite-Size Character Traits

Resources   Picture book: Rosenthal, Amy K. 1996. *Cookies: Bite-Size Life Lessons.* New
York: HarperCollins.

Chalkboard or whiteboard

Overhead projector and transparency of "Character Traits" list (provided in
the appendix)

Paper and drawing supplies

Bookbinding supplies

Procedure   Rosenthal's *Cookies: Bite-Size Life Lessons* features several feelings/traits
within the context of making, eating, and sharing cookies. Here's a representa-
tive page: "MODEST means you don't run around telling everyone you make
the best cookies, even if you know it to be true."

Read the picture book to students. During the reading, focus on the words
that are feelings/traits: *cooperate, patient, proud, modest, respect, trustworthy,
fair, unfair, compassionate, greedy, generous, pessimistic, optimistic, polite, honest,
courageous, envy, loyal, open-minded, regret, content, wise.*

When finished reading, write the lines from any page on the board,
such as:

> *MODEST means you don't run around telling everyone you make the
> best cookies, even if you know it to be true.*

Ask students to use the words from the page as a clue about what the word
in capital letters means. Allow student volunteers to provide synonyms, descriptions, and examples.

Then ask students to think about another setting or scenario, such as playing baseball. Ask students to think of an example in that setting or scenario that
could explain what the word in capital letters means. Record the responses on
the board, revising the example until students are pleased with it. Students
might answer with something similar to:

> *MODEST means you don't remind the poor fellow who strikes out
> every time that you hit a homerun every time you are at bat.*

Once students demonstrate their understanding of the concept, place
them in small groups. Display on a transparency the "Character Traits" list provided in the appendix. Ask the groups to select five traits each or assign traits to
them. (Perhaps the class needs a review on some traits or is learning new traits,

or maybe some traits are connected to another activity the students are working on in class.)

Decide on a setting or scenario to think about, such as camping. Then allow students to use paper and drawing supplies to author and illustrate five pages of their own *Bite-Size Life Lessons* book.

Assessment   Have groups present their book pages to the class. Students should talk about what the trait means and how they came up with the example. As needed, provide more discussion or examples to help students develop a deep understanding of the traits' meanings. Groups may need to revise their pages based on the discussion. When finished, bind their pages into a book for the classroom library.

Character/Graphic Organizers

Real People, Real Traits

Resources   Overhead projector and transparency of the Benjamin Franklin graphic organizer (provided in the appendix)
Picture book: Adler, David A. 1990. *A Picture Book of Benjamin Franklin.* New York: Holiday House.
Biographical picture books (suggestions provided)
Copier and paper
"Character Traits" list (provided in the appendix)
Posterboard and drawing supplies

Procedure   Prepare by making a transparency of the Benjamin Franklin graphic organizer (provided in the appendix).

Display the transparency of the graphic organizer, but do not discuss it. Begin reading aloud Adler's picture book about Benjamin Franklin. At appropriate points, pause to show how the traits and examples from the book are represented on the web. When finished, review the web again, making sure students understand how the information is presented.

Place students in small groups. Assign or allow each group to select one biographical picture book. (Some of Adler's picture books are suggested at the end of this activity. You might also choose picture books about topics the students are presently studying in social studies or that illustrate particular themes.)

Photocopy for each group the "Character Traits" list (provided in the appendix). Ask students to read their picture book, and as they do, to think of character traits from the list that match how the author describes the person in the book. Instruct students to use posterboard and drawing supplies to create a web with traits and examples as they read, similar to the one presented about Benjamin Franklin.

Assessment　　As groups are working, circulate to listen in on and add to the conversation. When groups are finished, allow students to present their webs to the class and discuss the traits and examples they included.

Suggested Picture Books　　Adler, David A. 1989. *A Picture Book of Abraham Lincoln.* New York: Holiday House.

————. 1990a. *A Picture Book of Benjamin Franklin.* New York: Holiday House.

————. 1990b. *A Picture Book of Martin Luther King, Jr.* New York: Holiday House.

————. 1992. *A Picture Book of Helen Keller.* New York: Holiday House.

————. 1993. *A Picture Book of Frederick Douglass.* New York: Holiday House.

————. 1994. *A Picture Book of Sojourner Truth.* New York: Holiday House.

————. 1995. *A Picture Book of Rosa Parks.* New York: Holiday House.

————. 1998. *A Picture Book of Louis Braille.* New York: Holiday House.

————. 2001a. *A Picture Book of Lewis and Clark.* New York: Holiday House.

————. 2001b. *A Picture Book of Sacagawea.* New York: Holiday House.

————. 2003. *A Picture Book of Harriet Beecher Stowe.* New York: Holiday House.

Student Samples　　Fourth graders Mossie and Garrett work independently to organize their thoughts after a read-aloud of Adler's (1994) *A Picture Book of Sojourner Truth.* See the figures that follow.

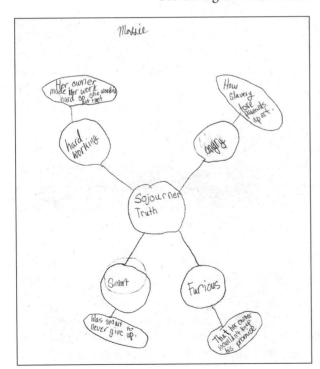

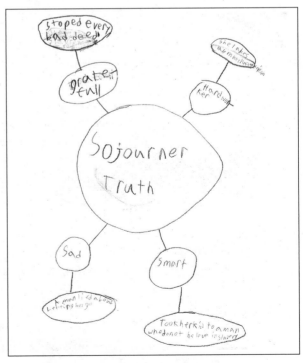

FIGURE 15　Mossie selects *hardworking, angry, furious,* and *smart,* and includes events from the book to support them.

FIGURE 16　Garrett jots down examples that show Sojourner Truth as grateful, hardworking, smart, and sad.

Plot/Setting/Graphic Organizers

The What and the Where

Resources   Picture book: Noble, Trinka. H. 1987. *Meanwhile Back at the Ranch.* New York: Penguin Puffin.
Chalkboard or whiteboard

Procedure   Read Noble's *Meanwhile Back at the Ranch* to students. As you do, use the tone of your voice to make the events in the two settings stand out, taking a disinterested tone for the events in the city and a cheerful tone for the events at the farm.

Then draw the following chart on the board (or use another graphic form that students might need experience with):

What Happens (Plot)	Where It Happens (Setting)
* * * *	In the City
* * * *	On the Ranch

Read the book again. This time, allow student volunteers to fill in the graphic with the major events of the story.

After the second reading of the book, ask students to discuss the differences between the events that happen in the city and on the ranch. Guide students into seeing the importance of the two settings to the story's plot. Specifically, students should be able to conclude (by using the information on the chart) that only dull things happen to the farmer while he is in the city, but exciting things happen on the ranch while he is away.

Extension   Provide students with the opportunity to explore the relationship between plot and setting in other picture books in the classroom library or those that have been used during read-alouds recently.

For further practice with graphic organizers, you might select stories in which multiple settings contribute to other story elements, such as plot or conflict. Through small-group and class discussions, students can gain practice articulating how various story elements are linked.

Theme

And the Theme Is

Resources   Display board materials
Markers
Construction paper
Tape

Procedure   Create a display board in which a variety of themes are listed. These themes could be: individualism, overcoming challenges, importance of family, working together, being strong in times of difficulty, and so on. You might also display the themes and examples featured in Chapter 5.

Show students the display board and discuss the meaning of each theme, providing many real-life examples as needed to ensure that students understand every theme.

After read-alouds and as students read texts in partnered and self-selected reading, have them decide if a certain theme on the display board is exemplified in a particular text.

Provide markers and construction paper, and ask students to write the book title and a description of how the text illustrates a particular theme. Have students tape the paper beneath the appropriate theme. (Students should add new themes as needed.) In addition, students might decide to include an illustration of a major plot event or write out a memorable quotation.

If appropriate, introduce the notion that texts might illustrate multiple themes and have students create more than one product for a particular book title.

Assessment   At various points throughout the year, review those books that are clustered under a particular theme. By rereading and discussing the books grouped around a common theme, students can further discuss how the stories do or do not relate to the chosen theme. Allow students to revise their papers and positions on the display board as necessary.

CHARACTER TRAITS

active	curious	horrible	respected
adventurous	daring	humorous	sad
afraid	delighted	ill	satisfied
alone	demanding	imaginative	scared
amazed	dependent	immature	secretive
ambitious	desperate	independent	selfish
amused	determined	innocent	sensible
angry	disappointed	inspired	serious
annoying	dishonest	intelligent	shocked
anxious	eager	interested	shy
appreciative	embarrassed	joyful	sick
ashamed	encouraged	kind	silly
astonished	excited	lazy	skilled
awed	fair	lonely	smart
bashful	fearful	lucky	sorry
bewildered	fearless	mad	startled
bold	forceful	mean	strong
bored	fortunate	motivated	stubborn
bossy	frantic	mysterious	stunned
bothered	frightened	negative	sure
bothersome	frustrated	nervous	surprised
brave	funny	nice	suspicious
bright	furious	noble	thoughtful
calm	generous	particular	thoughtless
careful	giving	patient	thrilled
careless	glad	perplexed	timid
caring	gloomy	picky	tired
certain	gracious	plain	troubled
chatty	grateful	playful	trustworthy
cheerful	greedy	pleased	truthful
childish	guilty	positive	uncertain
clever	happy	practical	unfair
concerned	hardworking	proud	unhappy
confident	hateful	pushy	unkind
content	honest	puzzled	unsure
courageous	honorable	quiet	upset
cowardly	hopeful	regretful	weak
creative	hopeless	relaxed	worried

Activities for Literary Techniques

Various Literary Techniques

The Big Book of Figurative Language

Collecting examples of figurative language techniques provides students with anchor examples they can call up when they encounter figurative language items on reading tests.

Resources   Picture book: Wiles, Deborah. 2001. *Freedom Summer*. New York: Simon and Schuster.
Paper and drawing supplies
Bookbinding supplies

Procedure   Announce that over a certain period of time, the class will be working to create a "big book" of figurative language. Tell students that you will explain the process, and then they will complete the first pages of their book after reading *Freedom Summer*.

Part One: The Process

Explain to students that they will contribute pages to the book by recording instances of figurative language they encounter during read-alouds and self-selected reading. Instruct students to record the phrase/sentence, where it was found, what it means, and what type of figurative language it is (for example, simile, metaphor, personification). Additionally, ask students to add an illustration for each instance of figurative language they contribute to the book. (Often, the illustrations will stick in students' minds and may further help them recall these anchor examples.)

Part Two: Creating Pages

Read the picture book *Freedom Summer*, stopping at the end of each page to allow students to identify and discuss any figurative language. Some examples follow.

Then allow students to work individually or in pairs to use paper and drawing supplies to contribute their own pages to the "big book" by recording and illustrating examples from *Freedom Summer*. Model the task, as shown here.

Model   Talk students through what one page might look like:

> "We churn that water into a white hurricane. . . ."
> Found in *Freedom Summer* by Deborah Wiles
> Meaning: The boys churned the water quickly until it swirled like a hurricane.
> Type: Hyperbole
> (Illustration)

Examples from the picture book that students might select for their pages include the following:

Hyperbole: *We shoot marbles in the dirt until we're too hot to be alive.*
Simile: *He crawls like a catfish, blows bubbles like a swamp monster. . . .*
Simile: *He smells like pine needles after a good rain.*
Simile: *John Henry says I smell like a just-washed sock.*
Hyperbole: *"This means war," I shout.*
Hyperbole: *"We churn that water into a white hurricane. . . ."*
Simile: *Then we float on our backs and spout like whales.*
Simile: *I wiggle in my chair like a doodlebug.*
Simile: *His face is like a storm cloud.*
Personification: *We can hear the breeze whisper through the grass.*

Assessment   Allow individuals or pairs to share their pages. As they share, make sure that students can define the type of figurative language they have identified (for example, hyperbole is exaggeration) and can explain why the example constitutes figurative language (for example, the water isn't actually turned into a hurricane).

Extension   In addition to inviting students to contribute pages on their own during self-selected reading, select specific times for all students to work towards contributing pages to the "big book." During these times, provide a collection of picture books that contain figurative language. (Use the resource below for suggestions.)

Give students the opportunity to share the pages they create with the class. Review the definitions of certain types of figurative language as well as other examples that have been collected.

Just before a reading assessment, take apart the "big book" and distribute the pages to the students who created them. Have each student use some of the pages to assemble a personal book of anchor examples that he or she intends to keep in mind during a reading test.

Resource for Selecting Picture Books with Figurative Language

Hall, Susan. 1994. *Using Picture Storybooks to Teach Literary Devices.* Phoenix: Oryx.

Various Literary Techniques

Figuratively Speaking

Resources "Figurative Language Strips" (provided in the appendix)
Copier and paper
Chalkboard or whiteboard
Picture book: Nolen, Jerdine. 2003. *Thunder Rose*. Orlando: Harcourt.
Tape

Procedure Prepare by copying and cutting apart the "Figurative Language Strips" sheet (provided in the appendix). On the board, make four columns and write in these words, one per column: *Similes, Figurative Language/Metaphors, Personification, Hyperbole.*

Divide students into four groups. Give each group the appropriate strips (as designated on the sheet), but do not identify which kind of figurative language is represented by the strips. In other words, do not tell Group 1 that all of their examples are similes.

Read the picture book *Thunder Rose* to the class. Tell students to listen for the examples of figurative language that are written on their strips.

Read the book a second time, this time stopping at the end of each right-hand page. Using the teacher's guide at the end of this activity, read off the examples of figurative language that appear on the pages you just read. Ask one member of each group to bring those strips to you. Place a piece of tape on the back of each strip and ask the students to put the examples in the correct columns. If students have difficulty, use definitions for the literary techniques to help them make a determination, such as "Does the example use the words *like* or *as*?" or "Does the example give a human quality to a nonhuman thing?" (Over time, students should realize that all of the examples in a particular group are of the same literary technique.

Continue until the reading is completed and all examples have been placed in their correct columns. Review the displayed examples by allowing group members to discuss why all of their strips are examples of a particular literary technique.

Teacher's Guide

End of Page 1: "Hailing rain, flashing lightning, and booming thunder pounded the door, inviting themselves in for the blessed event." [personification]

End of Page 2: [none]

End of Page 3: ". . . a lullaby . . . echoing since the beginning of time." [hyperbole]

"Rose snored up plenty that first night breathing on her own, rattling the rafters on the roof right along with the booming thunder." [hyperbole]

"She seemed determined to be just as forceful as that storm." [simile]

End of Page 4: ". . . Rose woke up hungry as a bear in spring . . ." [simile]

"No other newborn had the utter strength to lift a whole cow clear over her head and almost drink it dry." [hyperbole]

"She was as pretty as a picture . . ." [simile]

End of Page 5: [none]

End of Page 6: "Rose ran lightning-fast toward the herd . . . vaulted into the air and landed on the back of the biggest lead steer . . ." [hyperbole]

". . . landed on the back of the biggest lead steer like he was a merry-go-round pony." [simile]

End of Page 7: ". . . as playful as a kitten . . ." [simile]

End of Page 8: [none]

End of Page 9: "The mighty sun was draining the moisture out of every living thing it touched." [hyperbole]

"Even the rocks were crying out." [personification]

"Those clouds stood by and watched it all happen. They weren't even trying to be helpful." [personification]

End of Page 10: ". . . time seemed to all but stand still . . ." [metaphor]

". . . it's like a disease that's catching . . ." [simile]

End of Page 11: "They [the clouds] didn't take kindly to someone telling them what to do. And they were set on creating a riotous rampage all on their own." [personification]

". . . she became the only two-legged tempest to walk the western plains." [metaphor]

End of Page 12: "Is this the fork in the road with which I have my final supper?" [metaphor]

"Will this be my first and last ride of the roundup?" [metaphor]

". . . merciless . . . windstorm . . ." [personification]

". . . the winds joined hands . . ." [personification]

". . . she lifted her heart . . ." [metaphor]

"It [her song] rang from the mountaintops. It filled up the valleys." [hyperbole]

"It flowed like a healing river . . ." [simile]

End of Page 13: "And, gentle as a baby's bath, a soft, drenching-and-soaking rain fell." [simile]

". . . reaching into her own heart to bring forth the music that was there . . ." [metaphor]

". . . she had even touched the hearts of the clouds." [metaphor]

End of Page 14: "The stories of Rose's amazing abilities spread like wildfire, far and wide." [simile]

Metaphor

"I Am" Metaphors

For students who have trouble with identifying metaphor in texts, writing an "I Am . . ." paragraph could help them to see that metaphor is a direct comparison—*I* compared to *something else*. A memorable personal comparison provides students with an anchor example that they can recall when encountering items about metaphor on a reading assessment.

Resources Chalkboard or whiteboard
Overhead projector and transparency listing metaphor examples (provided in the Procedure section)
Paper and drawing supplies
Bookbinding supplies

Procedure   If desired, begin with a review of metaphor, perhaps collecting examples from texts that have been recently shared with the class.

Tell students that they will write about themselves by expanding on a metaphor. Provide the following list on the board and add to it as a class.

I am a butterfly.
I am sunshine on a cloudy day.
I am a night owl.
I am a walking encyclopedia.
I am a speed demon on my roller blades.
I am a tornado on the football field.

Model the task, as shown below. Then provide paper and drawing supplies so that each student can write an expanded metaphor and illustrate it.

Model   Place the following examples on a transparency and discuss:

- *I am a walking encyclopedia. I am filled with information of all kinds. Just ask me!*
- *I am a fifth-grade caterpillar. All year long I am in the cocoon of elementary school. At the end of the year, I develop wings and fly away to become a middle school butterfly.*

If necessary, have students work in groups to create a metaphor with the words "Our class is . . ." before asking students to work independently.

Assessment   Have students share their work with the class. Assess understanding and reteach as necessary. Add the metaphor pages to the class's "big book" of figurative language (see the activity on pages 198–199).

Extension   Emphasize the distinction between simile and metaphor by asking students to discuss how their metaphors can be turned into similes.

Personification

Pick Two, Any Two

Personification often hinges on attributing a human quality or action (the verb) to a nonhuman or abstract thing (the subject). Students should be able to scrutinize the subjects and verbs of sentences in order to recognize personification. A memorable anchor example will help students when encountering personification items on a reading assessment.

Resources   Chalkboard or whiteboard
Overhead projector and transparency of "Nonhuman Subjects" and "Human Verbs" sheet (provided in the appendix)
Paper and drawing supplies

Procedure   Write these examples of personification on the board and read them aloud:

- *Dirty dishes cried out from the kitchen for my brother to wash them.*
- *The stars refused to show up for work last night.*
- *The tree welcomed the tree house by hugging it with branches.*
- *The earthquake swallowed the town in one quick gulp.*

Ask volunteers to explain why the sentences are examples of personification. (Possible answers: Dishes can't cry; stars can't refuse to show up; a tree can't welcome or hug anything; an earthquake can't swallow.) Help students see that the verbs are actions that can be attributed to humans only, not nonhuman things.

Show a transparency of the nonhuman subjects and human verbs (provided in the appendix). Place students in pairs.

Provide drawing supplies. Ask each pair of students to write and illustrate an example of personification by selecting one subject and one verb and then adding more description, as in the examples on the board.

Assessment When pairs are finished working, ask volunteers to read their examples of personification. Have other students comment on why the statement is an example of personification. Allow students to rewrite to correct any statements that are not examples of personification. Add the personification pages to the class's "big book" of figurative language (see the activity on pages 198–199).

Student Samples The figures that follow show some fourth graders' examples of personification. Lauren's mountain cradled (Figure 17), Orion's rain ran and whispered (Figure 18), Ryann's stars huddled (Figure 19), and Sarah's tornado danced (Figure 20).

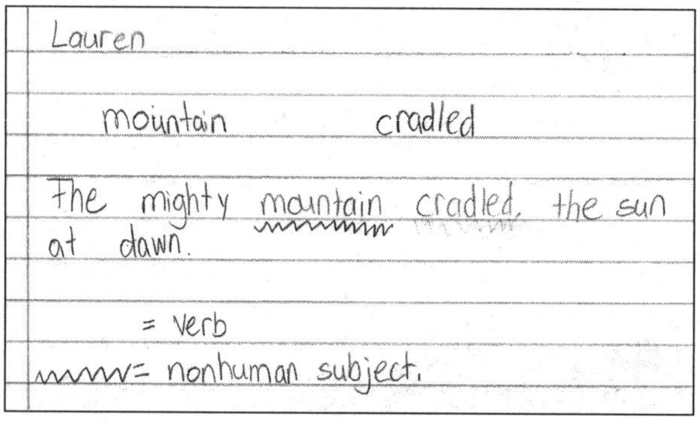
Lauren
mountain cradled
The mighty mountain cradled the sun at dawn.
= verb
~~~~ = nonhuman subject.

FIGURE 17

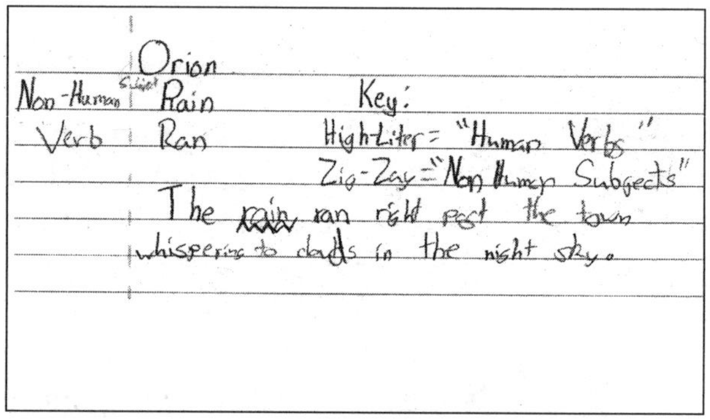
Orion
Non-Human Subject Rain
Verb Ran
Key:
High-Liter = "Human Verbs"
Zig-Zag = "Non Human Subjects"
The rain ran right past the town whispering to clouds in the night sky.

FIGURE 18

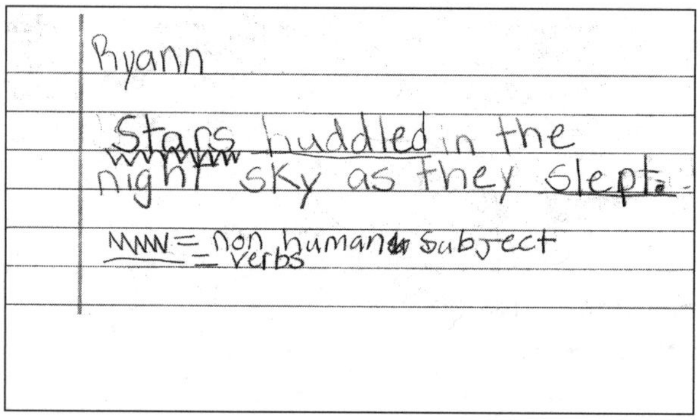
Ryann
Stars huddled in the night sky as they slept.
~~~~ = non human subject
___ = verbs

FIGURE 19

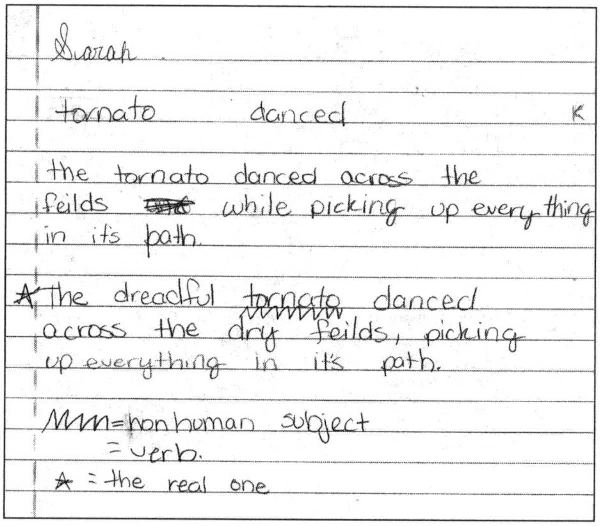
Sarah
tornato danced
the tornato danced across the feilds while picking up every thing in its path.
★ The dreadful tornato danced across the dry feilds, picking up everything in its path.
~~~~ = non human subject
= verb.
★ = the real one

FIGURE 20
~~~~

Hyperbole

For Real?

Resources
"Hyperbole Sentences" (provided in the appendix)
Copier and paper
Scissors
Chalkboard or whiteboard
Paper and drawing supplies
Bookbinding supplies
Tape

Procedure
Prepare by copying, cutting apart, and scrambling the "Hyperbole Sentences" sheet (provided in the appendix). Make enough sets so that when the class is divided into small groups, each group will have one complete set.

Begin by reviewing hyperbole. Write these examples on the board:

- *I love the movie* Enchanted. *I've memorized every word.*
- *I'm so tired. I could sleep for a decade.*

Ask volunteers to tell why the second sentence in each example is a hyperbole. (Possible answers: "I've memorized every word" is an exaggeration of how well the person knows the movie. "I could sleep for a decade" is an exaggeration of how long the tired person could actually sleep.)

Divide students into small groups. Provide each group with a set of examples from the "Hyperbole Sentences" sheet.

Ask the groups to sort the sentences into pairs so that the second sentence in each pair is an example of hyperbole, just as in the examples on the board.

Assessment
When the groups are finished, allow students to share their pairings and discuss why the second sentence is an example of hyperbole. Focus on the specific words that provide exaggeration (for instance, the words *two days* in the first example and the words *a hundred* in the second example).

Extension
Using the sentences on the left side of the "Hyperbole Sentences" sheet, students should work in pairs to create an original example of hyperbole (for instance, students can use the sentence *Marissa really loved the movie*, but they will need to replace the hyperbole sentence that accompanies it with an example of their own). Have students record, illustrate, and discuss their examples as a class. Then add them to the class's "big book" of figurative language (see the activity on pages 198–199).

Alliteration

Do Go On

Resources   Picture book: Edwards, Pamela D. 1996. *Some Smug Slug.* New York: HarperCollins.
Chalkboard or whiteboard
Paper and drawing supplies

Procedure   Read the picture book aloud. At the beginning, ask students what they notice. Accept and discuss the responses. When a student notices the use of the letter *s* at the beginnings of words, introduce or review the term *alliteration*. Throughout the remainder of the read-aloud, draw attention to the use of alliteration.

When finished reading, show the page that reads: "'Show-off,' scolded a squirrel, storing nuts for the season." Write the sentence on the board. Call on student volunteers to come up and underline the first letter of a word that contributes to the alliteration. Because there are five words beginning with *s*, five students should have the opportunity to participate.

Divide students into small groups. Provide paper and drawing supplies. Tell students that their challenge is to write a sentence about any animal that contains alliteration in four or five words. Ask students to underline the first letter of the words that contribute to the alliteration and to include an illustration. Model an example as shown below, if needed.

Model   Demonstrate the process for completing the task by asking a student to think of an animal. For example, a student might choose *cat*.

Ask students to brainstorm related words with that beginning letter. For example, students might offer *curious* and *cried*.

Then begin constructing a sentence with these words and others that are contributed. For example, students might say, "The curious cat cried when the mousetrap clamped his claw."

Check for understanding before allowing groups to begin their work together.

Assessment   Have the groups share their sentences. Draw attention to the alliteration by asking groups to point to the alliterative words.

Add the alliteration pages to the class's "big book" of figurative language (see the activity on pages 198–199).

Student Samples   A variety of animals found their way into third graders' examples of alliteration. See the figures that follow.

FIGURE 21 Paul, Mariela, and Johanna look into the life of a Louisiana lizard.

FIGURE 22 Angelica, Marina, and Moises set their sights on a San Antonio seal.

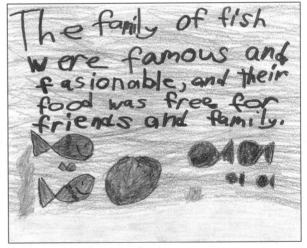

FIGURE 23 Saige focuses on a famous family of fish.

Activities for Interpretations

Cause-Effect

This Leads to That

Resources   "Cause-Effect Diagrams" (provided in the appendix)
Chart paper
Picture book (optional): Numeroff, Laura. 1985. *If You Give a Mouse a Cookie.* New York: HarperCollins.
Markers
Index cards
Tape
Chalkboard or whiteboard

Procedure   Prepare by copying the graphics from the "Cause-Effect Diagrams" sheet (provided in the appendix) onto chart paper, one diagram per sheet.

Begin by reviewing the relationship of cause and effect, drawing attention to the notion that one event can cause another thing to happen as a result. If needed, use a picture book to provide examples, such as *If You Give a Mouse a Cookie.*

Place students in small groups. Give each group one of the sheets of chart paper and a marker. Explain to students that a cause has been provided. Ask students to brainstorm for some of the possible effects. Tell students that they can be wildly imaginative and funny or realistic and serious about their responses.

Assessment   When all groups are finished, have one group come up to the front of the room with their chart paper folded so that no one can see it.

Ask the group to announce only the cause that they worked with. Then have the other students in the class guess some of the effects this group might have written on the chart paper.

After soliciting several responses, allow the group at the front of the room to reveal the effects they wrote on the chart paper. Prompt the group members to discuss how they came up with their effects. Compare their responses to those contributed by the class.

Continue this process until all groups have shared their work.

Extension   Throughout a typical school day, make a note of important events. Then use index cards to record one cause or one effect on each card. An example might be that the class does well on a math test (cause), so the teacher compliments the class or gives a reward/privilege (effect). The next day, have students work in small groups or as a class to match the causes and effects of the previous day.

Have students tape the *cause* index cards on the left side of the board and the corresponding *effect* index cards on the right side of the board. Draw an arrow between them to emphasize graphically that causes lead to effects.

Conclusion/Inference

"I Am" Inferences

Resources   Chalkboard or whiteboard
Various items to conduct charades (specified below)
Overhead projector and transparency of "I Am" inference example (specified in the Procedure section)
Writing or drawing supplies
Picture book (optional): Raschka, Chris. 1993. *Yo! Yes?* New York: Scholastic.

Procedure   **Part One: Charades**
On the board, make a two-column chart and give the two columns the headings "What I Know" and "What I Can Infer."

Explain the procedure for a version of charades that you will host. Tell students that you will act out a common, everyday action or movement. For example, tell students that if you put your finger over your lips, they can infer that you are asking them to quiet down. Instruct students to raise their hands when they know what you are doing. Tell students that they should first describe what you are doing (for example, "My teacher put her finger over her lips") and then say what can be inferred from the action (for example, "My teacher wants the class to be quieter").

As students respond, write their action descriptions under "What I Know" and their inferences under "What I Can Infer." (Remind students that they make inferences when they use what they see, read, and know in order to draw a conclusion about something.)

The chart that follows gives some example actions to act out (left side) and anticipates what inferences students might make (right side).

What I Know	*What I Can Infer*
My teacher put on a jacket.	*My teacher is cold.*
My teacher yawned.	*My teacher is sleepy (or tired or bored).*
My teacher is limping.	*My teacher's foot is hurt.*
My teacher is carrying an umbrella.	*My teacher is going somewhere where it is raining or might rain.*
My teacher is shaking and rubbing her hand.	*My teacher's hand fell asleep.*

Part Two: "I Am" Inferences

Divide students into small groups. Tell students that they will create "I Am" descriptions of something without identifying the thing by name. Give students suggestions for something they might describe—a favorite food, a particular job, an article of clothing, a nursery rhyme or favorite classroom book, and so forth. Remind students to use the five senses—taste, touch, smell, sound, and sight—to describe the thing.

Write the following example on a transparency. Show only one line at a time and pause after each line to elicit guesses.

> *I am used mostly during the day.*
> *I am larger than the other ones in the room.*
> *I allow papers and books to be stacked on top of me.*
> *I have drawers to hold things.*
> *I am found in classrooms and am very important to the teacher.*
> *I am . . .*

Students should guess that the example describes a teacher's desk. Ask students how each line supports their inference that the thing is a teacher's desk. To show more examples, use the student samples at the end of this activity.

Have students work in groups to select their thing and write a description. Remind students not to reveal the name of their thing in the description itself. If desired, students can provide an illustration and complete the statement "I am . . . [insert name of thing]" on the back of their papers.

Assessment   When they are finished, ask students to share their work with the class by reading one line at a time, just as in the model above, and allowing their classmates to guess. Ask students to discuss how the descriptions provided information that helped them make their inferences.

Extension   Use wordless picture books or picture books with limited text to continue showing students how inferences are made. For instance, Raschka's *Yo! Yes?* has few words, but students can make inferences to know how two boys form a friendship. A chart, similar to the one for charades, can be made to list "What I See" and "What I Can Infer."

Student Samples   Third graders' descriptions of their "I Am" things really put listeners' inference skills to work. See the figures that follow.

Brooks
Reanna MaTTew
I am like a stick.
I am strong.
I have leaves.
You need a macheti to break
or cut me.
I am found in parts of
Asia.
People eat me.
I am used to build houses.
I am found in many parts of
Asia....

I am ...

FIGURE 24 Brooks, Reanna, and Matthew's description is definitely challenging. Only after several details does *bamboo* come to mind!

Cheyanne
Shaiyanna
Madison
I am used almost all the time.
I am brocken some times.
I am have dffent colors.
I am chewed on some time.
I have dffent despgn.
If i'm used alot my top is gone.
MY teacher lpke my badge to say number 2.

FIGURE 25 Cheyanne, Shaiyanna, and Madison's details about the eraser help listeners know that they are describing a *pencil*.

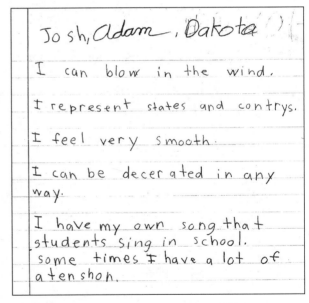

Josh, Adam, Dakota
I can blow in the wind.
I represent states and contrys.
I feel very smooth.
I can be decerated in any way.
I have my own song that students sing in school.
some times I have a lot of atenshon.

FIGURE 26 Josh, Adam, and Dakota describe both the appearance and the meaning of a *flag*.

Fact/Opinion

School Facts and Opinions

When opinions are mixed with facts in passages, opinions can be especially difficult for younger readers to detect. This activity requires students to use what they know about facts and opinions to distinguish the two on a variety of familiar topics.

Resources   Marker
Index cards
Chart paper
Tape
Chalkboard or whiteboard
Highlighters

Procedure   Prepare by using a marker to write one fact about a topic on one index card and one opinion about the same topic on another index card. These two index cards form a pair for that topic. Make pairs for at least five topics. Then make five sets of those pairs. Use the following topics, facts, and opinions to make the pairs (or make your own about topics presently being studied in class):

Topic	Fact	Opinion
Cafeteria	On Monday, (fill in food) was/were served.	I think our cafeteria's food is delicious.
Principal	Our principal was born in (fill in city).	Our principal is the best in the whole state.
School	Our school is located at (fill in address).	Our school building looks (fill in description, such as "new").
Teacher	One of the second-grade teachers is named (fill in name).	My second-grade teacher was always in a good mood.
Homework	(Teacher's name) does not assign homework on Fridays.	My math homework is much harder than my reading homework.

On five sheets of chart paper, make a chart that shows the topics but leaves blank spaces for the facts and opinions. Each piece of chart paper should look like the following (or should be adjusted according to whatever topics you use):

Topic	Fact	Opinion
Cafeteria		
Principal		
School		
Teacher		
Homework		

Divide students into five groups. Provide each group with one sheet of the prepared chart paper, tape, and one set of the index cards you've prepared. Instruct students to tape one fact and one opinion on the chart paper for each topic. Remind students to use key words in the statements to help them make their determinations. (If desired, review opinion words or definitions and examples of facts and opinions before beginning.)

Assessment   When all groups have had an opportunity to tape their facts and opinions to their chart paper, post the work from all groups on the board. Discuss the facts and opinions that are correct and incorrectly matched, adjusting the cards if necessary. Then ask volunteers from each group to highlight words in the statements that help them know that they are either facts or opinions.

Extension   Ask groups to write one fact and one opinion about any topic on index cards. (Students could use available texts in the classroom, such as magazines, newspapers, and novels.) Allow groups to trade cards and decide which statement is the fact and which is the opinion. Have groups share their responses with the class.

Supporting Evidence

Sentence Search

Supporting evidence items on reading assessments essentially task students to support a conclusion or big idea with specific evidence from the passage. Usually the correct answer is the idea or sentence that stands out in a meaningful way rather than is some insignificant detail. In this activity, students are asked to select a sentence that is important in the text and to tell why that sentence is significant.

Resources   Various print sources
Chalkboard or whiteboard
Paper and drawing supplies

Procedure   Tell students that people can remember lines from songs, movies, or speeches because they stand out in some way. Explain that some lines are memorable because they're funny or sad; other lines are memorable because they represent a truth that people can relate to. Share these examples:

- "The only thing you're going to be king of is king of the stupids!" from *Shrek the Third*. (It makes you laugh.)
- "Be who you are and say what you feel because those who mind don't matter and those who matter don't mind." from Dr. Seuss. (It makes you think.)
- "I think I can." from *The Little Engine That Could*. (It inspires you.)

Divide students into pairs or small groups. Decide if students will work with one assigned text (if students are presently working in book clubs, for instance) or with a variety of self-selected texts.

Ask the groups to read or reread a certain chunk of text (for example, an entire poem or one chapter of a novel) and pick out a favorite sentence that stands out as important.

Place these questions on the board and ask students to discuss them as they work together:

- Why did I pick this sentence?
- What big idea does the author want this sentence to show?

Ask students to use paper and drawing supplies to (1) illustrate their selected sentence, (2) write the sentence from the text beneath the illustration, and (3) record their answers to the two questions written on the board.

Assessment   Give students the opportunity to share their work with the class. Focus the discussion on what the sentence(s) means, what the text contributes to certain story elements (for example, plot, character, theme), what the author wants readers to think about, and so forth.

Extension   Devote a section of a bulletin board to collecting more memorable lines that students find in print throughout the year. Periodically, allow students to discuss those that they have contributed to the collection.

Student Samples   Third graders, while reading Beverly Cleary's *The Mouse and the Motorcycle* (1990) and discussing author's craft, choose important sentences from Chapter 10 to illustrate and ponder. See the figures that follow.

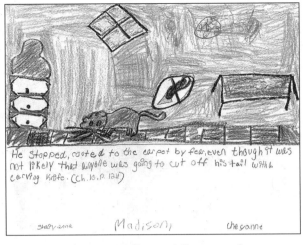

He stopped, rooted to the carpet by fear, even though it was not likely that anyone was going to cut off his tail with a carving knife. (Ch. 10, p. 124)

Shaiyanna   (Madison)   Cheyanne

FIGURE 27 Shaiyanna, Madison, and Cheyanne make a connection between their selected sentence and the author's reference to "Three Blind Mice."

Shaiyanna   madison
Cheyanne

(1) We picked this sentence because...
You have to think about it and it is a wounderful picture to draw.

(2) The big idea that the author

wants to show here is...
He wants to add a fairy tail which is the three blined mice.

adam   Josh   Dakota

"It's not that kind of awful" said Keith "I feel awful in a differentway. sort of in my insides" ch. 10 p. 108

adam
Josh   Da Kota

(1) I picked this sentence becuase. It would be intersting to figuer out why he is sike.

(2) The big idea that the author wants to show here is.
How people can feel bad inside.

FIGURE 28 Adam, Josh, and Dakota pick a sentence that makes them think about the author's intended meaning.

Activities for Text Matters

Author's Purpose

What's the Purpose?

Students will recognize in this activity that a topic can be written about for many purposes and that word choice is often a key to identifying an author's purpose. On a state assessment, students can access an author's purpose item by paying attention to the author's use of language as well as the text type and organizational structure.

Resources   "Purposes and Examples" sheet (provided in the appendix)
Copier and paper
Scissors
Theme-based magazines (optional)

Procedure   The "Purposes and Examples" sheet (provided in the appendix) features author purpose words (left side) that often appear on reading assessments and examples of text that fit with each purpose (right side).

Copy the page, cut apart the twelve boxes, and scramble them. Make four sets this way.

Divide students into four groups. Distribute a set of purposes and examples to each group. Ask groups to match the purpose word with the corresponding example.

Assessment   When groups are finished, call on various groups to tell which example was matched to each purpose word you call out.

Then have students identify the key words that helped them determine which purpose and example fit together. The words underlined below might be selected and discussed by groups; if not, lead a discussion to draw attention to these words.

Describe	Camp Townsend is located on the banks of a <u>sparkling blue</u> river and <u>nestled</u> between <u>two beautifully wooded</u> mountains.
List	Each camper is responsible for <u>the following: snacks and water, hiking boots, a fishing pole, a backpack, and a sleeping bag.</u>
Persuade/Convince	You <u>must</u> join us this weekend; <u>don't miss out</u> on an <u>adventure of a lifetime.</u>
Inform	Camp Townsend is <u>located 45 miles south of Boston.</u> A map <u>will be provided</u> in your <u>camping information packet.</u>
Entertain	Anything that could go wrong did go wrong the summer I attended Camp Townsend. <u>The story goes something like this . . .</u>
Explain	<u>First, put the poles together to make the frame</u> of the tent. <u>After</u> the frame is together, <u>put the cover on</u> it. The cover should fit snugly. If not, <u>check the directions again</u> to make sure the frame is properly put together.

Extension   Extend the focus on key words that indicate an author's purpose by selecting magazines that are theme based. Have students comb through the articles and other information to find examples of different purposes, including the six purpose words in this activity as well as others you have introduced and discussed in class.

Text Type

You Name It!

Because students need familiarity with various text types that are included on most state reading assessments, the suggested texts can be studied as anchor examples.

Resources   Various texts (suggestions provided)
Chalkboard or whiteboard
Sticky notes
Markers
Construction paper
Tape

Procedure   Collect the suggested texts identified in the teacher's guide that follows. Add other texts, if desired.

Use the second column of the teacher's guide to list on the board the text types of the books you provide. (Do not list the source or evidence!)

Place students in groups. Provide groups with a few of the collected books, sticky notes, and markers. Ask them to flip through the pages and look for features that help them know what type of text each book is. Have the groups record the title and their choice of the text type (from those listed on the board) on a sticky note.

When all groups are finished with the first set of books, ask groups to trade book sets. Repeat the process until all groups have seen and responded to every book.

While students are working, use a marker to write each text type on a sheet of construction paper. Tape the pieces of paper throughout the room or on the board.

Assessment   When the groups have finished working, ask them to place their sticky notes (with the title and text type written on them) to the piece of construction paper of the same text type.

Then discuss each text type individually by determining if all groups identified the same title. Call on one group to talk about the features they noticed that helped them make their decisions. Use the evidence ideas in the third column of the teacher's guide to steer the discussion.

Teacher's Guide

Source	Text Type	Evidence
Koi and the Kola Nuts: A Tale from Liberia by Verna Aardema	Folktale	Is about a particular group of people.
The Persian Cinderella by Shirley Climo	Fairy tale	Begins "Long ago"; is a variation of a tale told over centuries; involves magic; a character transforms.
The Little Red Ant and the Great Big Crumb: A Mexican Fable by Shirley Climo	Fable	Animals can talk; teaches a moral.
Doña Flor: A Tall Tale About a Giant Woman with a Great Big Heart by Pat Mora	Tall tale	Events with some truth to them have been mixed with exaggerations over time.
Atalanta's Race: A Greek Myth by Shirley Climo	Myth	A human has superhuman characteristics.
Moonflute by Audrey Wood	Fantasy	A moonbeam transforms into a flute; a person has the power to fly.
The Garden of Abdul Gasazi by Chris Van Allsburg	Mystery	Some events and the story's ending cannot be explained.
Through My Eyes by Ruby Bridges	Nonfiction/Informational/ Autobiography	True events are told by the person who lived them.
Roberto Clemente: Pride of the Pittsburgh Pirates by Jonah Winter	Biography	Describes important true events in one person's life.
So, What's It Like to Be a Cat? by Karla Kuskin	Interview	Answers provided to a question.
More Than Anything Else by Marie Bradby	Historical fiction	True events about a real person are told with a fictionalized perspective.
A Writing Kind of Day: Poems for Young Poets by Ralph Fletcher	Poetry	Several poems of different types make up a collection; some have short lines.

Author's Organization

Putting Together How Ideas Are Put Together

Because students need familiarity with various organizational patterns that are assessed on most state reading tests, the suggested texts can be studied as anchor examples.

Resources Various texts (suggestions provided)
Chalkboard or whiteboard
Sticky notes
Markers
Construction paper
Tape

Procedure Collect the suggested texts identified in the teacher's guide that follows. Add other texts, if desired.

Use the second column of the teacher's guide to list on the board the organizational pattern of the books you provide. (Do not list the source or evidence!)

Place students in groups. Provide groups with a few of the collected books, sticky notes, and markers. Ask them to flip through the pages and look for features that help them know how the author organizes the ideas. Have the groups record the title and their choice of the organizational pattern (from those listed on the board) on a sticky note.

When all groups are finished with the first set of books, ask groups to trade book sets. Repeat the process until all groups have seen and responded to every book.

While students are working, use a marker to write each organizational pattern on a sheet of construction paper. Tape the pieces of paper throughout the room or on the board.

Assessment When the groups have finished working, ask them to place their sticky notes (with the title and organizational pattern written on them) to the piece of construction paper of the same organizational pattern.

Then discuss each organizational pattern individually by determining if all groups identified the same title. Call on one group to talk about the features they noticed that helped them make their decisions. Use the evidence ideas in the third column of the teacher's guide to steer the discussion.

Teacher's Guide

Source	Organizational Pattern	Evidence
The Day Jimmy's Boa Ate the Wash by Trinka Noble	Cause/effect	Each event leads to an effect or outcome.
Baseball Saved Us by Ken Mochizuki	Problem/solution	A problem is introduced and a solution is described.
So, What's It Like to Be a Cat? by Karla Kuskin	Interview—Question and Answer	A cat answers a boy's questions.
How to Bake an American Pie by Karma Wilson	Process	Steps are used to provide a recipe.
Meanwhile Back at the Ranch by Trinka Noble	Comparison/contrast	The story shifts between two settings during the same time period.
Grandfather's Journey by Allen Say	Chronological	Major events in the author's grandfather's life are told in sequence.
Diary of a Spider by Doreen Cronin	Chronological—Diary form	Dates are used to indicate entries in the spider's journal.
Amazing Book of Questions and Answers by John Guest	Nonfiction—Question and answer	A series of questions are posed and answered.
LaRue for Mayor: Letters from the Campaign Trail by Mark Teague	Multiple text types—Letters mixed with newspaper articles	Letters and newspaper articles are used to tell about a dog that runs for mayor.

Conclusion

Of the many fine and funny children's books about standardized tests, Judy Finchler's (2000) *Testing Miss Malarkey* must be my favorite. In it, teacher Miss Malarkey bites her nails as "THE TEST" approaches. The principal orders No. 2 pencils and demands that they are perfectly sharpened. The cafeteria serves fish because it's good for the brain. The art teacher helps students color in circles to get them ready for marking answers. Even the narrator's mother takes on the frenzied frame of mind; after she reads the narrator a bedtime story, she assigns a worksheet to be completed before he sleeps.

But among these laugh-out-loud moments in the book is a single sentence that, for some schools, is too real to be funny: "The closer we got to 'THE TEST DAY,' the weirder things got."

The fact that things get weirder as the testing window approaches actually makes sense, unfortunately. Consider this: If tests could truly mirror quality instruction and if testing conditions could replicate the collaborative atmosphere that is so important in classrooms, then teachers wouldn't actually need to address "the test" with their students at all; test day could come and go and things would not get weird. But that's not what happens with testing. Tests are different from essentially every other activity that takes place in schools. That's why things get weird.

I think this notion has to be addressed with students explicitly. After all, it must seem odd to them that for many months each school year, they engage with texts and are encouraged to share openly and think broadly about the ideas in those texts, but during test week, they are told not to look around, not to ask around, not to share, and not to think divergently. They must narrow their views. They must limit possible interpretations to a correct one, as deemed by some anonymous test writer.

Students need to be privy to honest discussions about tests to minimize their confusion and anxiety about them. They need opportunities to feel prepared and competent not just as learners in classrooms but also as test takers. Confidence comes as a result of a deep awareness of test formats, test language, test tasks, and other test features that affect students' ability to demonstrate what they know about reading.

Intentions and Reflections

Eliminating students' confusion and anxiety. Helping students feel prepared and competent. Increasing students' confidence. Providing opportunities for students to demonstrate what they know. These are all my main goals in writing this book.

It is my hope that the various sections and chapters of this book are the beginnings of the ideas, and sometimes the very words, that teachers can share with students. Section 1 seeks to disavow teachers and students of myths about testing, mostly because some of those myths—when acted upon—can negatively affect students' scores.

Section 2 aims to help teachers familiarize students with the content of most reading tests; after all, students cannot fully demonstrate what they know when they are nervous and uncertain about what they will encounter on a test. I tried to fill this section with helpful approaches to taking reading tests, from developing familiarity with item types to having a variety of reading and test-taking strategies that are easy to use.

Section 3 is intended to provide teachers with high-quality content typical of a traditional reading test—materials that might spark rich and lively discussions about test features, tasks, and strategies. The passages and items in this section will, in all hopes, open up opportunities for students to voice their understandings to teachers and for teachers to seize those moments to clarify and develop their students' conceptions.

Section 4 endeavors to supply teachers with engaging activities to strengthen the skills that students will have to demonstrate on most reading tests. As the classroom's decision maker and guide, the teacher can decide how best to present the ideas in the activities—modifying, modeling, and extending the concepts to meet their students' needs. The products that students create as a result of completing the activities further provide teachers with access to students' understandings of various reading skills and strategies.

The content of this book grew and grew as I kept returning to the title: *What Every Elementary Teacher Needs to Know About Reading Tests*. The pages in this book represent what I believe is the most important and most useable knowledge for teachers.

Moving Forward and Staying Informed

There are many opportunities that exist beyond this book for teachers to complement and increase their knowledge of tests and testing. One source is email lists that are tailored to providing specific information that is important to you. Your state department's curriculum and assessment divisions, for example, might have email lists that will deliver valuable information to your email inbox. Staying connected to the curriculum and assessment divisions means being reassured that you are being provided with the latest information regarding your state's testing program.

Another source is professional reading organizations that allow members to join email lists that relate specifically to their teaching positions and areas of interest.

Perhaps the best way to stay informed is to visit your state department of education's website. These websites are usually well maintained. Released tests, sample item booklets, and various testing information bulletins can be downloaded from the sites. Because information is made available at various points throughout the school year, it is important to visit regularly.

Letting Your Voice Be Heard

Teachers can and should have their voices heard—within the walls of their school as well as across the state.

On the local level, share. If you've had years of experience with testing and have learned a few things the hard way, share with those around you who are eager to listen. If you feel in the dark about matters related to testing, listen to those around you who are eager to share. Form a discussion group and work chapter by chapter through this book and others that address topics that are important to you. Agree, disagree, and exemplify your opinions with your classroom experiences.

On the state level, volunteer. State assessments cannot be developed without teacher input. State departments of education seek teachers to volunteer to serve on various committees—from deciding which standards should be assessed in a new testing program to determining which items are appropriate for inclusion on a field test or live administration. In addition to contributing what you know, you will have the opportunity to learn from fellow educators and to receive information directly from the state department staff who host these meetings (rather than having to depend on other, sometimes less reliable, channels).

✓ ✓ ✓

Finally, I suppose I should address the elephant in the room. While it is my experience as a test developer that qualified me most for writing this book, it has not been lost on me that readers may think that my experience in the industry inevitably makes me a proponent of testing. The simple truth is that I do think that assessments of various types can provide useful data, but I also know that test scores are being valued presently on local, state, and national levels in ways that fall far outside the purposes and legitimacy of those tests.

I want teachers to have the information in this book so that tests are less powerful, not more powerful. I want this book to be a resource for teachers to draw on during their delivery of high-quality instruction, not a prescriptive plan that reduces classrooms to dens of test practice. I want teachers to decide what they think their students should know about reading tests and to decide how students should receive that information so that they feel informed, prepared, competent, and capable.

Knowledge about reading tests wipes out their mystery. Knowledge of reading tests keeps the weirdness away. Knowledge about reading tests prevents the further confiscating of valuable instructional time with students.

Neither teacher nor child should feel defenseless as the test day arrives.

Appendix

Vocabulary Development

Antonym Squares

Guilty	Hardworking	Appreciative
confident	lazy	serious
innocent	caring	startled
anxious	determined	ungrateful

Confident	Joyful	Disappointed
uncertain	immature	imaginative
sorry	gloomy	weak
joyful	smart	pleased

Perplexed	Selfish	Trustworthy
wondering	generous	upset
hopeless	worried	dishonest
sure	frustrated	stubborn

Chatty	Nervous	Timid
tired	calm	shy
quiet	mysterious	regretful
shocked	fearful	adventurous

Satisfied	Interested	Playful
displeased	silly	encouraged
suspicious	bored	serious
startled	inspired	fortunate

Cowardly	Dull	Greedy
innocent	nervous	boring
brave	lonely	lucky
anxious	imaginative	kind

What Every Elementary Teacher Needs to Know About Reading Tests (From Someone Who Has Written Them) by Charles Fuhrken. Copyright © 2009. Stenhouse Publishers.

Answer Key for Antonym Squares

Guilty	Hardworking	Appreciative
confident	lazy ✔	serious
innocent ✔	caring	startled
anxious	determined	ungrateful ✔

Confident	Joyful	Disappointed
uncertain ✔	immature	imaginative
sorry	gloomy ✔	weak
joyful	smart	pleased ✔

Perplexed	Selfish	Trustworthy
wondering	generous ✔	upset
hopeless	worried	dishonest ✔
sure ✔	frustrated	stubborn

Chatty	Nervous	Timid
tired	calm ✔	shy
quiet ✔	mysterious	regretful
shocked	fearful	adventurous ✔

Satisfied	Interested	Playful
displeased ✔	silly	encouraged
suspicious	bored ✔	serious ✔
startled	inspired	fortunate

Cowardly	Dull	Greedy
innocent	nervous	boring
brave ✔	lonely	lucky
anxious	imaginative ✔	kind ✔

Synonym/Antonym Cards

Synonyms	Antonyms
cold-shivering	hot-cold
sleepy-tired	wet-dry
start-begin	empty-full
excited-eager	dirty-clean
nice-kind	love-hate
hurry-rush	lost-found
easy-simple	easy-hard
angry-mad	messy-neat
hurt-injured	calm-nervous
big-large	huge-tiny
quick-fast	loud-quiet

Breakup Cards

Attentive	Showing attention
Cheerful	Full of cheer
Curiosity	Having a curious quality
Decoration	The results of being decorated
Discomfort	Not having comfort
Disharmonious	Not having harmony
Dreadful	Full of dread
Evaluation	The results of measuring the worth of something
Fragment	The result of breaking
Gloomy	Having gloom
Gradually	In a gradual manner
Harmless	Without harm
Hesitation	The action of hesitating
Imperfection	The results of not being perfect
Impossible	Not possible
Inscription	The results of writing in or on something

Breakup Cards *(continued)*

Invisible	Not able to be seen
Irresistible	Not able to be resisted
Knowledgeable	Having knowledge
Meaningless	Having no meaning
Memorial	Something made or done to remember a person or event
Nonsense	Without sense
Peacefully	In the manner of having peace
Portable	Able to be carried
Preview	To view before
Rewind	To wind again or back
Spectacle	Relating to looking or seeing
Telegram	A written message sent from a distance
Unacceptable	Not able to accept
Unapproachable	Not able to approach
Unashamed	Not ashamed
Unbelievable	Not able to be believed

What Every Elementary Teacher Needs to Know About Reading Tests (From Someone Who Has Written Them) by Charles Fuhrken. Copyright © 2009. Stenhouse Publishers.

Important Ideas

Story Windows

Story Cards

Frank has a job delivering newspapers in his neighborhood. Because dogs like to chase him, Frank carries a long stick that he waves at them while he hollers, "Shoo. Get away, dog." But one time that stick got caught in his front tire. The bike wobbled, and Frank went flying over the top of his handlebars. He landed with a thud. After that, he decided that maybe just hollering "Shoo. Get away" was enough to keep the dogs away. He never carried a long stick again.

Do you know the story about the tortoise and the hare? The tortoise challenges the hare to a race. The hare, being fast, is confident he will win. Along the way, he stops to nibble some grass and to take a nap. Meanwhile, the tortoise keeps a steady pace. Eventually, the tortoise crosses the finish line and wins. The moral of this story is that anything can be accomplished if you just keep trying at it.

Schools sometimes host an event called Career Fair. During a career fair, people from the community come to talk about their jobs. Students get to ask questions about those jobs. It helps students think about the kinds of jobs they might be interested in when they are adults.

Breakfast is said to be the most important meal of the day. After a good breakfast, the brain starts to wake up and students can concentrate on their work. Without a good breakfast, the brain stays asleep and students have a hard time staying focused. What kind of breakfast did you have today?

Do you know of a place called Easter Island? There, huge stone faces can be found. No one knows for sure what they mean or why the people who lived on the island long ago made them. Easter Island remains a mystery.

What Every Elementary Teacher Needs to Know About Reading Tests (From Someone Who Has Written Them) by Charles Fuhrken. Copyright © 2009. Stenhouse Publishers.

Literary Elements

"Pick Three"

Afraid	Calm	Mad
frightened scared bold fearful	patient amazed relaxed quiet	dishonest angry upset furious

Bright	Troubled	Pushy
smart intelligent brilliant unkind	lucky concerned worried bothered	lonely bossy bold demanding

Brave	Caring	Content
daring courageous mysterious heroic	considerate kind immature thoughtful	pleased happy satisfied skilled

Cheerful	Confused	Bashful
glad positive timid joyful	strong bewildered puzzled perplexed	shy quiet timid stubborn

Motivated	Astonished	Unhappy
eager determined sensible inspired	startled smart shocked stunned	upset embarrassed gloomy sad

Ashamed	Excited	Hateful
patient embarrassed regretful guilty	eager intelligent thrilled happy	mean unkind horrible determined

What Every Elementary Teacher Needs to Know About Reading Tests (From Someone Who Has Written Them) by Charles Fuhrken. Copyright © 2009. Stenhouse Publishers.

Answer Key for "Pick Three"

Afraid frightened scared ~~bold~~ fearful	**Calm** patient ~~amazed~~ relaxed quiet	**Mad** ~~dishonest~~ angry upset furious
Bright smart intelligent brilliant ~~unkind~~	**Troubled** ~~lucky~~ concerned worried bothered	**Pushy** ~~lonely~~ bossy bold demanding
Brave daring courageous ~~mysterious~~ heroic	**Caring** considerate kind ~~immature~~ thoughtful	**Content** pleased happy satisfied ~~skilled~~
Cheerful glad positive ~~timid~~ joyful	**Confused** ~~strong~~ bewildered puzzled perplexed	**Bashful** shy quiet timid ~~stubborn~~
Motivated eager determined ~~sensible~~ inspired	**Astonished** startled ~~smart~~ shocked stunned	**Unhappy** upset ~~embarrassed~~ gloomy sad
Ashamed ~~patient~~ embarrassed regretful guilty	**Excited** eager ~~intelligent~~ thrilled happy	**Hateful** mean unkind horrible ~~determined~~

Character Traits

active	curious	horrible	respected
adventurous	daring	humorous	sad
afraid	delighted	ill	satisfied
alone	demanding	imaginative	scared
amazed	dependent	immature	secretive
ambitious	desperate	independent	selfish
amused	determined	innocent	sensible
angry	disappointed	inspired	serious
annoying	dishonest	intelligent	shocked
anxious	eager	interested	shy
appreciative	embarrassed	joyful	sick
ashamed	encouraged	kind	silly
astonished	excited	lazy	skilled
awed	fair	lonely	smart
bashful	fearful	lucky	sorry
bewildered	fearless	mad	startled
bold	forceful	mean	strong
bored	fortunate	motivated	stubborn
bossy	frantic	mysterious	stunned
bothered	frightened	negative	sure
bothersome	frustrated	nervous	surprised
brave	funny	nice	suspicious
bright	furious	noble	thoughtful
calm	generous	particular	thoughtless
careful	giving	patient	thrilled
careless	glad	perplexed	timid
caring	gloomy	picky	tired
certain	gracious	plain	troubled
chatty	grateful	playful	trustworthy
cheerful	greedy	pleased	truthful
childish	guilty	positive	uncertain
clever	happy	practical	unfair
concerned	hardworking	proud	unhappy
confident	hateful	pushy	unkind
content	honest	puzzled	unsure
courageous	honorable	quiet	upset
cowardly	hopeful	regretful	weak
creative	hopeless	relaxed	worried

What Every Elementary Teacher Needs to Know About Reading Tests (From Someone Who Has Written Them) by Charles Fuhrken. Copyright © 2009. Stenhouse Publishers.

Sample Web for Benjamin Franklin

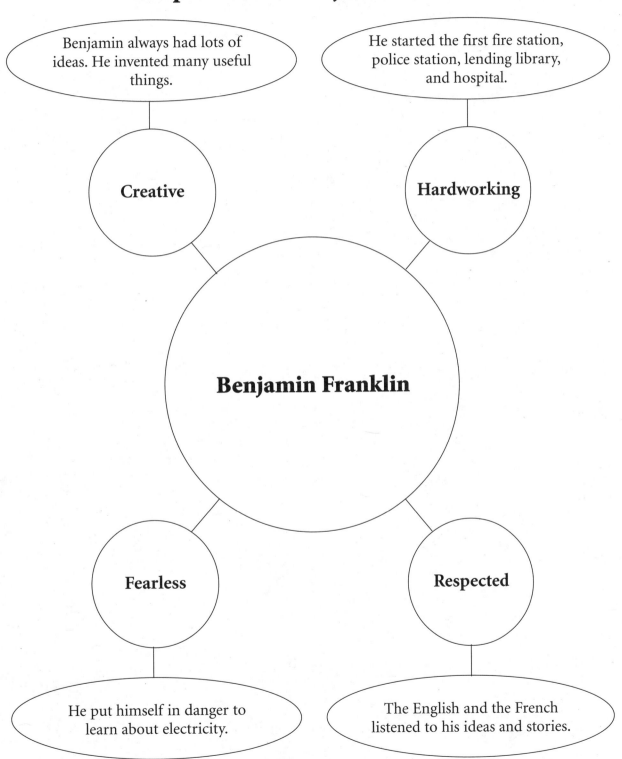

Benjamin always had lots of ideas. He invented many useful things.

He started the first fire station, police station, lending library, and hospital.

Creative

Hardworking

Benjamin Franklin

Fearless

Respected

He put himself in danger to learn about electricity.

The English and the French listened to his ideas and stories.

Details from: Adler, David A. 1990. *A Picture Book of Benjamin Franklin*. New York: Holiday House.

Literary Techniques

Figurative Language Strips

Group 1: Similes

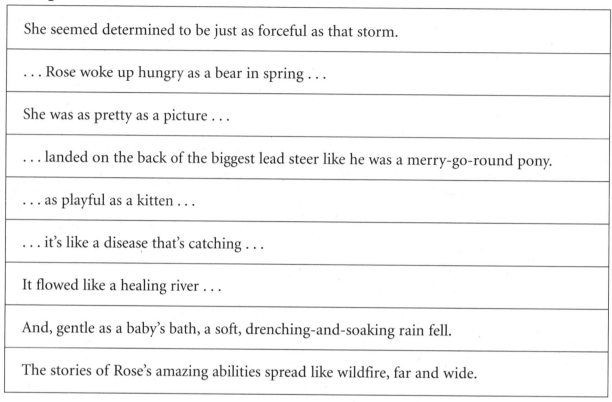

She seemed determined to be just as forceful as that storm.

. . . Rose woke up hungry as a bear in spring . . .

She was as pretty as a picture . . .

. . . landed on the back of the biggest lead steer like he was a merry-go-round pony.

. . . as playful as a kitten . . .

. . . it's like a disease that's catching . . .

It flowed like a healing river . . .

And, gentle as a baby's bath, a soft, drenching-and-soaking rain fell.

The stories of Rose's amazing abilities spread like wildfire, far and wide.

Group 2: Figurative Language/Metaphors

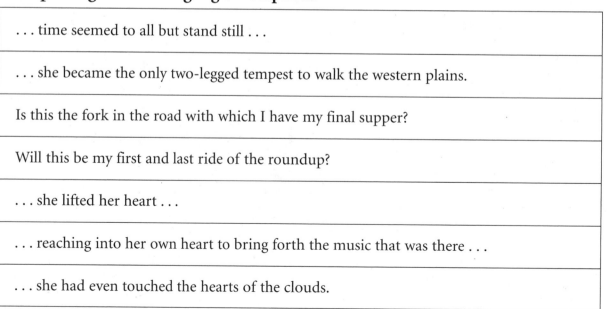

. . . time seemed to all but stand still . . .

. . . she became the only two-legged tempest to walk the western plains.

Is this the fork in the road with which I have my final supper?

Will this be my first and last ride of the roundup?

. . . she lifted her heart . . .

. . . reaching into her own heart to bring forth the music that was there . . .

. . . she had even touched the hearts of the clouds.

Group 3: Personification

Hailing rain, flashing lightning, and booming thunder pounded the door, inviting themselves in for the blessed event.
Even the rocks were crying out.
Those clouds stood by and watched it all happen. They weren't even trying to be helpful.
They [the clouds] didn't take kindly to someone telling them what to do. And they were set on creating a riotous rampage all on their own.
. . . merciless . . . windstorm . . .
. . . the winds joined hands . . .

Group 4: Hyperbole

A lullaby . . . echoing since the beginning of time.
Rose snored up plenty that first night breathing on her own, rattling the rafters on the roof right along with the booming thunder.
No other newborn had the utter strength to lift a whole cow clear over her head and almost drink it dry.
Rose ran lightning-fast toward the herd . . . vaulted into the air and landed on the back of the biggest lead steer.
The mighty sun was draining the moisture out of every living thing it touched.
It [her song] rang from the mountaintops. It filled up the valleys.

Nonhuman Subjects and Human Verbs

Nonhuman Subjects	Human Verbs
thoughts	danced
ideas	whispered
truth	spoke
doubt	moaned
memories	cried
rain	called out
breeze	ate
wind	awoke
clouds	slept
lightning	raced
thunder	skipped
tree	ran
hurricane	walked
tornado	hurried
fire	huddled
flames	shook
dessert	cradled
dirty dishes	wrapped
sun	agreed
moon	refused
stars	angered
sky	applauded
mountains	remembered

What Every Elementary Teacher Needs to Know About Reading Tests (From Someone Who Has Written Them) by Charles Fuhrken. Copyright © 2009. Stenhouse Publishers.

Hyperbole Sentences

Marissa really loved the movie.	She talked about it for two days without stopping.
That cookie recipe was too complicated.	It required about a hundred ingredients.
It was so cold yesterday.	Even the burning wood in the fireplace had icicles hanging from it.
The hurricane was brutal.	It blew our little Texas town into the state of Oregon.
I miss my grandmother so much.	I think of her two million times a day.
The librarian demands absolute silence in the library—or else!	Even a mouse is scared to go there.
My backpack has so much stuff in it.	I had to hire a professional weightlifter to carry it for me.
The play by Shakespeare was so boring.	The audience's snores were so loud that we couldn't hear the actors.
The ant colony in my back yard is huge.	The city has decided to give it a zip code.
The popcorn had too much butter on it.	I didn't get to eat a single bite because the popcorn kept slipping through my fingers.

Interpretations

Cause-Effect Diagrams

Cause	Effects
All the lights went out in the school.	→ → →
Cause	**Effects**
A tornado headed toward a family's house.	→ → →
Cause	**Effects**
Dad was bringing home a new puppy.	→ → →
Cause	**Effects**
A mouse ran across the classroom floor.	→ → →

What Every Elementary Teacher Needs to Know About Reading Tests (From Someone Who Has Written Them) by Charles Fuhrken. Copyright © 2009. Stenhouse Publishers.

Text Matters

Purposes and Examples

Describe	Camp Townsend is located on the banks of a sparkling blue river and nestled between two beautifully wooded mountains.
List	Each camper is responsible for the following: snacks and water, hiking boots, a fishing pole, a backpack, and a sleeping bag.
Persuade/Convince	You must join us this weekend; don't miss out on an adventure of a lifetime.
Inform	Camp Townsend is located 45 miles south of Boston. A map will be provided in your camping information packet.
Entertain	Anything that could go wrong did go wrong the summer I attended Camp Townsend. The story goes something like this . . .
Explain	First, put the poles together to make the frame of the tent. After the frame is together, put the cover on it. The cover should fit snugly. If not, check the directions again to make sure the frame is properly put together.

Calkins, Lucy, Kate Montgomery, and Donna Santman. 1998. *A Teacher's Guide to Standardized Reading Tests: Knowledge Is Power.* Portsmouth, NH: Heinemann.

Conrad, Lori L., Missy Matthews, Cheryl Zimmerman, and Patrick A. Allen. 2008. *Put Thinking to the Test.* Portland, ME: Stenhouse.

Downing, Steven M., and Thomas M. Haladyna. 2006. *Handbook of Test Development.* Mahwah, NJ: Lawrence Erlbaum.

Firestone, William A., Roberta Y. Schorr, and Lora F. Monfils. 2004. *The Ambiguity of Teaching to the Test: Standards, Assessment, and Educational Reform.* Mahwah, NJ: Lawrence Erlbaum.

Fuhrken, Charles, and Nancy Roser. Forthcoming. "Exploring High-Stakes Tests as a Genre." In *Teaching the Texts Children Need to Succeed on High-Stakes Tests and in the Classroom.* Ed. Barbara Moss and Diane Lapp. New York: Guilford.

Greene, Amy. H., and Glennon D. Melton. 2007. *Test Talk: Integrating Test Preparation into Reading Workshop.* Portland, ME: Stenhouse.

Hall, Susan. 1994. *Using Picture Storybooks to Teach Literary Devices.* Phoenix: Oryx.

Harvey, Stephanie, and Anne Goudvis. 2007. *Strategies That Work: Teaching Comprehension for Understanding and Engagement.* Portland, ME: Stenhouse.

Johnson, Genevieve. 1998. "Principles of Instruction for At-Risk Learners." *Preventing School Failure* 4 (2): 167–174.

Kohn, Alfie. 2000. *The Case Against Standardized Testing: Raising the Scores, Ruining the Schools.* Portsmouth, NH: Heinemann.

Pearson, P. David, and Margaret C. Gallagher. 1983. "The Instruction of Reading Comprehension." *Contemporary Educational Psychology* 8: 317–344.

Raphael, Taffy E. 1982. "Question-Answering Strategies for Children." *The Reading Teacher* 36: 186–190.

Serafini, Frank. 2004. *Lessons in Comprehension: Explicit Instruction in the Reading Workshop.* Portsmouth, NH: Heinemann.

Valencia, Richard R., and Bruno J. Villarreal. 2003. "Improving Students' Reading Performance via Standards-Based School Reform: A Critique." *The Reading Teacher* 56: 612–621.

Vygotsky, Lev S. 1978. *Mind in Society: Development of Higher Psychological Processes.* Cambridge, MA: Harvard University Press.

Literature

Aardema, Verna. 1999. *Koi and the Kola Nuts: A Tale from Liberia.* New York: Atheneum.

Adler, David A. 1989. *A Picture Book of Abraham Lincoln.* New York: Holiday House.

———. 1990a. *A Picture Book of Benjamin Franklin.* New York: Holiday House.

———. 1990b. *A Picture Book of Martin Luther King, Jr.* New York: Holiday House.

———. 1992. *A Picture Book of Helen Keller.* New York: Holiday House.

———. 1993. *A Picture Book of Frederick Douglass.* New York: Holiday House.

———. 1994. *A Picture Book of Sojourner Truth.* New York: Holiday House.

———. 1995. *A Picture Book of Rosa Parks.* New York: Holiday House.

———. 1998. *A Picture Book of Louis Braille.* New York: Holiday House.

———. 2001a. *A Picture Book of Lewis and Clark.* New York: Holiday House.

———. 2001b. *A Picture Book of Sacagawea.* New York: Holiday House.

———. 2003. *A Picture Book of Harriet Beecher Stowe.* New York: Holiday House.

Armstrong, Jennifer. 2003. *A Three-Minute Speech: Lincoln's Remarks at Gettysburg.* New York: Simon and Schuster.

Barrett, Judi. 2001. *Things That Are Most in the World.* New York: Aladdin.

Bradby, Marie. 1995. *More Than Anything Else.* New York: Orchard.

Bridges, Ruby. 1999. *Through My Eyes.* New York: Scholastic.

Charlip, Remy. 1993. *Fortunately.* New York: Aladdin.

Cleary, Beverly. 1990. *The Mouse and the Motorcycle.* New York: HarperCollins.

Cleary, Brian P. 1999. *A Mink, a Fink, a Skating Rink: What Is a Noun?* Minneapolis: Carolrhoda Books.

———. 2000. *Hairy, Scary, Ordinary: What Is an Adjective?* Minneapolis: Carolrhoda Books.

———. 2001. *To Root, to Shoot, to Parachute: What Is a Verb?* Minneapolis: Carolrhoda Books.

———. 2002. *Under, Over, By the Clover: What Is a Preposition?* Minneapolis: Carolrhoda Books.

———. 2003. *Dearly, Nearly, Insincerely: What Is an Adverb?* Minneapolis: Carolrhoda Books.

———. 2004a. *I and You and Don't Forget Who: What Is a Pronoun?* Minneapolis: Carolrhoda Books.

———. 2004b. *Pitch and Throw, Grasp and Know: What Is a Synonym?* Minneapolis: Carolrhoda Books.

———. 2006a. *A Lime, a Mime, a Pool of Slime: More About Nouns.* Minneapolis: Carolrhoda Books.

———. 2006b. *Slide and Slurp, Scratch and Burp: More About Verbs.* Minneapolis: Carolrhoda Books.

———. 2006c. *Stop and Go, Yes and No: What Is an Antonym?* Minneapolis: Carolrhoda Books.

———. 2007. *Quirky, Jerky, Extra Perky: More About Adjectives.* Minneapolis: Carolrhoda Books.

Clements, Andrew. 1996. *Frindle.* New York: Simon and Schuster.

Climo, Shirley. 1995a. *Atalanta's Race: A Greek Myth.* New York: Clarion.

———. 1995b. *The Little Red Ant and the Great Big Crumb: A Mexican Fable.* New York: Clarion.

———. 1999. *The Persian Cinderella.* New York: HarperCollins.

Cronin, Doreen. 2005. *Diary of a Spider.* New York: HarperCollins.

Curtis, Jaime L. 1998. *Today I Feel Silly and Other Moods That Make My Day.* New York: HarperCollins.

Cuyler, Margery. 1993. *That's Good! That's Bad!* New York: Henry Holt.

———. 2002. *That's Good! That's Bad! in the Grand Canyon.* New York: Henry Holt.

———. 2007. *That's Good! That's Bad! in Washington, DC.* New York: Henry Holt.

Edwards, Pamela D. 1996. *Some Smug Slug.* New York: HarperCollins.

Finchler, Judy. 2000. *Testing Miss Malarkey.* New York: Walker.

Fletcher, Ralph. 2005. *A Writing Kind of Day: Poems for Young Poets.* Honesdale, PA: Boyds Mills.

Frasier, Debra. 2000. *Miss Alaineus: A Vocabulary Disaster.* Orlando: Harcourt.

Grover, Max. 1997. *Max's Wacky Taxi Day.* Orlando: Harcourt.

Guest, John. 2003. *Amazing Book of Questions and Answers.* New York: Backpack Books.

Heller, Ruth. 1995. *Behind the Mask: A Book About Prepositions.* New York: Putnam.

———. 1998a. *A Cache of Jewels and Other Collective Nouns.* New York: Putnam.

———. 1998b. *Kites Sail Higher: A Book About Verbs.* New York: Putnam.

———. 1998c. *Many Luscious Lollipops: A Book About Adjectives.* New York: Putnam.

———. 1998d. *Merry-Go-Round: A Book About Nouns.* New York: Putnam.

———. 1998e. *Up, Up, and Away: A Book About Adverbs.* New York: Putnam.

———. 1999. *Mine, All Mine: A Book About Pronouns.* New York: Putnam.

Kuskin, Karla. 2005. *So, What's It Like to Be a Cat?* New York: Atheneum.

Mochizuki, Ken. 1993. *Baseball Saved Us.* New York: Lee and Low.

Mora, Pat. 1997. *Tomas and the Library Lady.* New York: Alfred A. Knopf.

———. 2005. *Doña Flor: A Tall Tale About a Giant Woman with a Great Big Heart.* New York: Alfred A. Knopf.

Most, Bernard. 1992. *There's an Ant in Anthony.* New York: HarperTrophy.

Noble, Trinka. H. 1980. *The Day Jimmy's Boa Ate the Wash.* New York: Puffin.

———. 1987. *Meanwhile Back at the Ranch.* New York: Penguin Puffin.

Nolen, Jerdine. 2003. *Thunder Rose.* Orlando: Harcourt.

Numeroff, Laura. 1985. *If You Give a Mouse a Cookie.* New York: HarperCollins.

Parish, Peggy. Amelia Bedelia series. New York: HarperTrophy.

Prelutsky, Jack. 1990. *Something Big Has Been Here.* New York: Greenwillow Books.

Pulver, Robin. 2006. *Nouns and Verbs Have a Field Day.* New York: Holiday House.

Raschka, Chris. 1993. *Yo! Yes?* New York: Scholastic.

Rosenthal, Amy K. 1996. *Cookies: Bite-Size Life Lessons.* New York: HarperCollins.

Say, Allen. 1993. *Grandfather's Journey.* Boston: Houghton Mifflin.

Teague, Mark. 2008. *LaRue for Mayor: Letters from the Campaign Trail.* New York: Scholastic.

Van Allsburg, Chris. 1979. *The Garden of Abdul Gasazi.* New York: Houghton Mifflin.

Walton, Rick. 2004. *Suddenly Alligator: An Adverbial Tale.* Salt Lake City: Gibbs Smith.

———. 2005a. *Bullfrog Pops.* Salt Lake City: Gibbs Smith.

———. 2005b. *Once There Was a Bull . . . Frog.* Salt Lake City: Gibbs Smith.

———. 2005c. *Why the Banana Split.* Salt Lake City: Gibbs Smith.

———. 2006. *Around the House the Fox Chased the Mouse: A Prepositional Tale.* Salt Lake City: Gibbs Smith.

Wiles, Deborah. 2001. *Freedom Summer.* New York: Simon and Schuster.

Wilson, Karma. 2007. *How to Bake an American Pie.* New York: Margaret K. McElderry.

Winter, Jonah. 2005. *Roberto Clemente: Pride of the Pittsburgh Pirates.* New York: Atheneum.

Wood, Audrey. 1986. *Moonflute.* San Diego: Harcourt.

Index

261